Bulk discounts available. For details visit:
www.amacombooks.org/go/specialsales
Or contact special sales:
Phone: 800-250-5308
Email: specialsls@amanet.org
View all the AMACOM titles at: www.amacombooks.org
American Management Association: www.amanet.org

This publication is designed to provide accurate and authoritative information in regard to the subject matter covered. It is sold with the understanding that the publisher is not engaged in rendering legal, accounting, or other professional service. If legal advice or other expert assistance is required, the services of a competent professional person should be sought.

Library of Congress Cataloging-in-Publication Data

Papke, Edgar.
  True alignment : linking company culture with customer needs for extraordinary results / Edgar Papke.
    pages cm
  Includes bibliographical references and index.
  ISBN-13: 978-0-8144-3336-2
  ISBN-10: 0-8144-3336-7
  1. Marketing. 2. Customer relations. 3. Corporate culture. I. Title.
  HF5415.P2384 2014
  658.8—dc23

                                                              2013027430

About AMA
American Management Association (www.amanet.org) is a world leader in talent development, advancing the skills of individuals to drive business success. Our mission is to support the goals of individuals and organizations through a complete range of products and services, including classroom and virtual seminars, webcasts, webinars, podcasts, conferences, corporate and government solutions, business books, and research. AMA's approach to improving performance combines experiential learning—learning through doing—with opportunities for ongoing professional growth at every step of one's career journey.

Printing number
10 9 8 7 6 5 4 3 2 1

TRUE ALIGNMENT

To Helmut and Christine Papke. Thank you for your perseverance, resilience, and courage . . . and never-ending love.

CONTENTS

PREFACE

This book represents the first time a comprehensive framework is provided for exploring in a simple way how we all participate in the art of business. It brings together in a comprehensive and understandable approach various aspects that are generally written about and presented separately, including the customer, product and market strategy, branding, organizational and team cultures, and leadership. This approach is easily applied to any business situation and ties together all the elements in a consistent view of what motivates us to engage in business in the ways we do. As a customer, employee, CEO, business leader, manager, or entrepreneur, you'll recognize yourself in this book.

True Alignment is also the first book to provide a measurable and observable approach to aligning the customer to a company's culture and what makes this distinctive relationship work. In writing this book, one of my goals is to provide a framework that can be applied to any aspect of business, allowing you to determine when alignment exists and when it doesn't. This includes how alignment affects whether you are satisfied or dissatisfied as a customer, a happy or an unhappy employee or team member, or a self-actualizing leader or entrepreneur in pursuit of a business strategy and culture that aligns to your personal motivations and influence.

Everything in life is personal and an aspect of our individual and shared human experience. As you read about the various aspects of alignment, you'll very likely find yourself exploring your own personal and intimate relationship to the art of business. As a result, I invite you to find new ways in which to see yourself and better understand the choices you are confronted with every day. And, why you make the decisions you do. My belief is that you will find this very empowering. At the very least, you'll find it thought provoking.

Another unique feature of this book is the range of examples providing insightful stories about how alignment leads to success. Often, business books focus on what makes larger organizations and corporations more competitive and successful, often leaving the reader with insights that are only useful within the context of larger companies and frequently only of use to those in leadership positions. Or, books focus on the more tactical aspects of entrepreneurial pursuits for the owners of smaller businesses or one-person companies. I have intentionally included examples of smaller companies and businesses, as well as those of some of major multinational corporations and brands you are familiar with. What you will find is that the alignment framework in this book applies to all businesses regardless of their size, market, and origin. This makes this book valuable to any reader, in any role.

Finally, this book is unique because of its timing. Over the last century, how we engage in the art of business has dramatically changed and has, as a result, changed our world forever. My sense is that this is a good time to examine how and why we've arrived at the business society of today, and how we can better prepare ourselves for the future. We are at a critical time. It is very likely that each of us has some level of distrust in our current relationship to business. I believe that we can realign our relationships to business and rediscover the trust required for the successful future of our business society.

By the time you reach the final pages, you'll likely conclude that alignment is the key to business success. Whether in the form of purpose, vision, strategy, branding, culture, and who we all are as customers, it is the most important conversation among businesses and their leaders, teams, and employees. This applies to everyone worldwide. Alignment is the ongoing conversation that leads to success. *Alignment is the conversation.*

That being said, welcome to the conversation.

ACKNOWLEDGMENTS

About fifteen years ago, a very talented friend of mine, Peter Arco-
mano, told me that I am a synthesist—a person capable of creating
new ways to see things through my observations and the fusion of different ideas, views, and subjects. It was a descriptive that I had not heard
before and, out of my respect for all his insights and the depth of our
friendship, it stuck with me. I've come to recognize that to write a book
like *True Alignment*, requires one to synthesize a broad range of ideas and
sources of knowledge.

The ideas and thinking that led to *True Alignment* are the result of
the work of the great thinkers, those without whose views on the world
of business and contributions I would not have found my path. In particular, they are the sages who have in one form or another shaped my
thinking on alignment and the study of organizational cultures. These
include Edgar Schein, Warren Bennis, Peter Drucker, Jim Collins, Rosa-
beth Moss Kanter, Stephen Covey, John Kotter, Tom Peters, and Peter
Senge. In particular, I am thankful to Bill Schneider, who as both a friend
and expert in organizational development, helped further my interest in
alignment and encouraged my exploration of cultures.

I will forever be grateful to the late Will Schutz for providing the insights into human behavior and motivation that have become a key contribution to the ideas that evolved into *True Alignment*. To this end, I am
also indebted to Ron Luyet for helping further Will's work. Ron is a gifted
teacher, and I am thankful for his support of my approaches to business
alignment and his encouragement in writing this book.

I have benefited greatly from a host of colleagues. Foremost among
them are Theresa Blanding and Bob Carrothers. Over the span of our
relationship, Theresa has patiently listened to me as my thoughts and
ideas evolved. I am grateful for her critique and ongoing encouragement
in finding the truth and simplicity of the art of business and the power of
alignment. She is also a priceless resource in working with the multitude

of clients and organizations with whom we have engaged. Bob and I spend invaluable hours in intimate conversation and exploration together. Along with also patiently listening to my thoughts, he has been an unrelenting supporter of my work, provides a constant reminder of its value, and is a positive force in my life. I'd like to give special thanks to my loving brother Dieter who, more than twenty-five years ago, guided me to the path of the work I do and helped me to trust my intuition and imagination.

I am also deeply grateful to the host of colleagues and friends who support my work. While there are far too many to include here, I would like to specifically thank Clyde Horner, Ozzie Gontang, Bill Oyler, Don Myers, Alison Whitmire, Peter Baiardi, John Walker, Bob Berk, Lynn Whitfield, Dick Shorten, Lance Descourouez, Karen O'Connell, John Nirenberg, Michael and Kiffie Hester, Rick Martin, Tom Lockwood, and Doug Gertner for their friendship and encouragement.

I am beholden to our clients and the over 1,000 CEOs and business leaders with whom I have the opportunity to interact every year in my presentations and workshops. They have provided an incredible resource for the application of my work and shared insights that continue to define how valuable alignment is. I cannot express enough my gratitude for letting me into their lives. I also am grateful to the over 15,000 CEO members of Vistage International and TEC, for letting me be a part of their wonderful community for the last twelve years and openly sharing their challenges in business and life, as well as their ideas, with me.

I'd like to thank my agent Maryann Karnich and express my my gratitude to Scott Edelstein for his help and guidance. To Christina Parisi, Michael Sivilli, Barbara Chernow, and the other members of the team at AMACOM Books, I wish to extend my sincere gratitude.

Lastly, I'd like to thank my wife Lori, our children Taylor, Trevor, Teagan and Taylor, my brother Lothar, and my parents Helmut and Christina for supporting, listening, encouraging, and believing in my pursuits. Your love has no boundaries.

*High-performing teams and organizations
are groups of aligned individuals committed to creating
extraordinary results for themselves and one another.*

TRUE ALIGNMENT

Introduction

It's All About Alignment

The key strategic imperative of any business is alignment.

A lignment has long been the greatest challenge of leadership. Its importance, along with its effect on performance, has only increased over time. Today, to come close to competing and succeeding in the chaotic and rapidly shifting business environment, leaders must create aligned teams and organizations.

For extraordinary companies—those that consistently compete and win in the marketplace—the overriding characteristic that is invariably present and separates them from their competition is alignment. And, because it is so important, the challenge is all the more difficult.

Most leaders, teams, and companies struggle with alignment because, until now, they lacked an effective and easy-to-apply framework and approach. As a result, they tackle individual aspects of business—such as vision, strategy, processes and systems, and culture—without aligning them. The following chapters will introduce you to the Business Code, a framework for alignment that can be applied to any organization or team, regardless of its size. It will show leaders and their companies how to confront and overcome the challenges of misalignment. The code also provides the tools needed to create strategies and initiatives and take actions that result in the alignment required to compete and achieve high levels of performance. The outcomes of applying this framework include:

- Alignment that clearly defines the trusted relationship of the business to the customer, the customer's expectation, and what the brand stands for.
- Alignment of leadership that is responsible for role modeling, reinforcing, and leading an aligned culture and is committed to the reputation and success of the business; leaders who hold themselves and other leaders responsible for their personal alignment to the organization, as well as its vision, and its culture.
- Alignment of goals and strategies across and down through organizations and teams, large and small, demonstrated by the contribution each group and team member makes to the organization's vision and strategies.
- Alignment of each individual to the values, beliefs, and expectations of the culture; each member knows how success is created at individual, group, and company-wide levels.
- Alignment that results in every person being responsible and acting in alignment with the business's intention, as conveyed through each member's commitment to the customer.
- Alignment that contributes to the resilience that great companies and teams demonstrate when confronted with difficult issues and challenges and keeps them from going off course or losing sight of their mission, vision, and intended outcomes.
- Alignment that is demonstrated through every decision and action taken by every member of the organization or team, how they fit into its culture, and what the company and team have promised to deliver to the customer.

THE DANGERS OF MISALIGNMENT

Most of us are all too familiar with the consequences of misalignment. We get caught up in the conflicts and blame games that result when everyone is not working toward the same outcome. Time and energy is wasted trying to overcome misalignments, which can disrupt and destroy teamwork and eventually bring down entire companies. The consequences of misalignment are grave. Among others, they include:

- A lack of focus on results that support the vision and strategy of the team and organization, resulting in poor performance.
- A lack of a shared and consistent approach to serving the customer, which damages the company's reputation and brand and creates customer distrust.
- A lack of the ability to leverage and fully utilize team members' individual talents and strengths, which decreases motivation and reduces their desire to contribute.
- A lack of clear expectations resulting in unmet performance requirements, poor accountability, distrust, and potentially divisive conflict.
- A lack of responsibility and mutual accountability among team members that results in the loss of trust and commitment to individual and team performance.
- A lack of open communication, resulting in finger pointing, poor conflict management, and dysfunctional behavior.
- A lack of aligned approaches to problem solving, decision-making, role definition, and processes and procedures, causing confusion and disengagement.
- A lack of teamwork among leaders that cascades through an organization, which results in conflict, an "us versus them attitude," and an inability to perform at the required level.

Clearly, misalignment *is costly*. Typically a negative financial impact results, which can be obvious or often hidden. Among the hidden costs are unmet goals and objectives; missed opportunities; missed sales; unmet promises to the customer; and a myriad other failures that result from dysfunction within a group, team, or company. One way or another, misalignment results in a failure, or a lack, of execution, which has a negative financial impact on a business.

All too often, leaders find themselves searching for answers to these problems without realizing that misalignment is at the root of them. They instead rely on hit-and-miss approaches and fixes, as well as temporary measures that provide only short-term solutions.

Obviously, the consequences of misalignment are too many and too powerful to ignore. Therefore, leaders must focus on the challenge of creating and leading aligned teams and organizations and view it as an opportunity to improve performance. Great leaders and team members actively seek out and confront misalignments.

THE PATH OF ALIGNMENT

Recognizing that alignment is the greatest challenge leaders face is only the beginning. The ongoing effort of aligning people to work together to contribute to and accomplish a set of shared outcomes and goals requires knowledge and well-developed leadership competencies. The most difficult job is managing and leading others.

At the root of the failure of organizations and teams to perform is the inability of people to work together in support of one another and their shared goals. No one accomplishes anything without the help of others and working together toward a shared goal requires alignment.

To begin effectively aligning and leading their organizations and teams, leaders must clearly and consistently address the what, why, and how of the company. If this were easily accomplished, being a great leader would be much less demanding, less difficult, and less valued. This is what makes alignment the single most important aspect of leading in today's complex and fast-changing world. Whether you are a CEO, business owner, manager, or team leader, it is not only your greatest challenge—it is your calling.

The what, the why, and the how are the three questions the Business Code addresses. Too often people are unclear about *what* they are contributing, are disengaged emotionally from *why* what they are doing it, and confused and fearful because they don't really understand *how* they are supposed to do it.

Extraordinary companies and teams are those in which the what, why and how are aligned.

- They have a clearly articulated and understood vision of *what* they want to accomplish. They know what the desired outcomes are and are able to innovate to continuously create and deliver a product or service that reflects and aligns with the customers' expectations.
- Their people are emotionally engaged because they know *why* what they're doing matters and the benefit it brings, believe in *what* is being

created and care deeply about it, and have a shared sense of purpose and feel responsible for their contribution to making it happen.

• They are aligned on *how* to work together to achieve results. They have a plan or strategy. More important, they know the steps in a process, system, or procedure and act in alignment with the values and beliefs of the organization or the team's culture.

For several reasons, *why* is currently getting the most attention. There is widespread concern over the lack of employee engagement in larger companies. A second, less obvious reason is that customers buy products or services to fulfill individual needs. To succeed, a business has to align those working for it to the emotional aspirations of the customer.

Today's complex and fast-paced world leads businesses to focus on finding a solution that offers the best return. It's much like getting someone's mindshare. This often keeps them from seeing that there's more they could do and benefit from. Last, as businesses and consumers, we seek greater meaning from what we produce, sell, and buy, and the significance these have to our quality of life, social benefit, and environmental impact. This, along with the abundance of options, leads us to look for less complex choices and simpler yet more powerful solutions.

Simplicity and alignment are not mutually exclusive. *When all three components of what, why, and how are present, a company or team works well. Leave one out, and things become complicated.* The alignment of the three is the true source of extraordinary performance. Place too much emphasis on one, and a leader will soon run into trouble. Therefore, leaders need to remember the importance of and pay attention to each. This begins with clearly communicating the "what"—the vision, goals, and outcomes the organization must accomplish to compete and be successful, defining and leveraging the emotional motivators of "why," and articulating the "how."

What: I often see leaders with a clear vision of *what* they want to accomplish. They articulate and share their vision and goals with the members of their company or team. They may even have a well-defined roadmap and lay out a set of measurable outcomes with key performance indicators intended to challenge their group. Yet people still don't take the initiative to get the job done.

When this happens, leaders are disappointed and wonder why the team doesn't exude the same energy and commitment that they do. They question why there is conflict among team members about who is responsible for what, who has the authority to make decisions, how roles are defined, or how people are expected to communicate and share information. They have a great idea of what they are supposed to do, yet they lack the emotional commitment and an understanding of how they will work together to achieve the intended outcome. The leader and team members are clear on the definition of *what*. However, they lack the emotional *why* and a description of *how* to work with one another.

Why: Throughout my career, I've coached many leaders who are able to charismatically engage others in a cause. They connect with and draw on people's emotional motivation. Unfortunately, a reliance on this component can result in a false hope that a shared sense of purpose and mission will emotionally engage people and result in success. The hope is that if there is meaning and everyone shares in *why*, *what* will organically emerge, and the team will find a way to work together to get it done.

While it's inspirational to believe that this can happen, it's rare for it to do so. In fact, when it is successful, some form of individual or shared leadership has usually emerged to provide a framework for the clear articulation of a measurable outcome and the steps needed to achieve it. More often, while everyone puts forward his or her own best intentions, the group has difficulty reaching consensus about what the members need to produce to best deliver the shared cause. The result is a lack of agreement and cohesion about *how* things are done. The group has the *why*, yet lacks the *what*, and therefore cannot know *how* to achieve it.

How: Over the last twenty years, leaders have learned to pay a attention to culture and go beyond the surface definition that it is about processes and systems. In addition, although most leaders appreciate the role of values and beliefs in defining culture, most still don't possess a framework for articulating, observing, or measuring it. Therefore, they can't intentionally lead their cultures.

This is important because *culture is the true how. It defines how people treat and work with one another,* including how they are expected to act and what is considered acceptable and unacceptable behavior. Culture provides the framework for how people live the values and beliefs of a group, how they gain and use power and influence, as well as how planning occurs, decisions get made, roles get defined, and conflicts are dealt with. It also explains their responsibility to one another. Culture holds the key to defining trust and respect.

Still, if leaders focus only on culture and expect the *what* and the *why* to emerge, they miss the other benefits of alignment. The leadership and a team or company that performs to its true potential must have an emotional and cognitive connection to what it intends to achieve and why it exists.

Because business is a human art, the why and how extend far beyond the processes, systems, and step-by-step actions people take to create and deliver a product or service competitively to the marketplace. At the core of the relationship between provider and buyer are the why and how of their emotional connection. This applies not just to the product or service , it also applies to the emotional affiliation the customer has to the organization's culture and its brand. When aligned, trust is manifested and sustained, and the provider enjoys the benefits of brand loyalty.

Alignment's power and influence also applies to the people responsible for delivering a competitive offering to the customer; it defines how they communicate, cooperate, and collaborate. It also provides the basis of the customer experience. How are a company's tenets of trust—its values and beliefs—expressed to the customer? The alignment of internal behavior to the external experience of the buyer results in loyalty that lies at the core of successful competition.

When leaders and team members focus on alignment, they connect and integrate the various elements that make a great business work, including aligning the intention to the customer and brand, vision and strategy, and the business's culture and how it is led. Whether it pertains to the customer relationship, service, product development, operational capability, or human resources, focusing on alignment engages leaders in questioning and challenging how strategies and initiatives support the organization.

Alignment is a key source of *innovation and creativity, the building of one idea upon another*. It creates an environment in which people communicate at broader and deeper levels and increases the opportunity for the exchange of ideas. When we leverage alignment across a team and organization, we take critical thinking and problem solving to higher levels, resulting in increased innovation, creativity, and better performance.

As we look to the future, learning to apply a framework for *alignment will continue to be the key skill and competency of great leaders.* Leaders can no longer focus on just one aspect of, or strategy for, change, or on a particular facet of product, service, or market development. This will become more evident and powerful if we are to successfully compete in a global marketplace in which the speed of change and complexity continues to grow.

This book offers an opportunity to assess and actualize the strategies that will enable you to better lead and contribute to the alignment of your organization and team. The Business Code provides insight into what motivates customers and how human needs are fulfilled. It will help you understand how brand intention provides the platform for the alignment of deliverables to the customer and how that entices the customer to buy and results in brand loyalty.

We'll then turn our attention to culture, a subject that challenges even the greatest of leaders and companies. We'll explore how the patterns and norms of behavior bring values and beliefs to life and guide organizations and teams in how they create and deliver a product or service to the customer. You'll discover how cultures are influenced and how to measure and observe the alignments and misalignments that hold back a team or company's ability to reach their desired levels of performance.

Next, we'll investigate the influence of leadership on brand intention, strategy, and culture and the importance that leadership development plays in successful alignment. What motivates leaders is key to understanding the dynamics of how team members engage one another and the customer.

Whatever your role—customer, contributor, employee, team member, leader, or CEO—you are influenced by alignment.

ONE

The Human Art of Business

Business is the most advanced form of human art.

We all engage in business. Every day, we take part in business. It may not be obvious, yet from the moment we wake, we are consumers—by turning on a light; running water; dressing; eating breakfast; gassing up the car; stopping for coffee; and, of course, texting and emailing. Throughout the day, you engage in activities that contribute to the creation and delivery of a product or service. By all accounts, business is the most advanced art form that we engage in. All other forms of art rely on the ability to create and do business. Without commerce, they are unable to sustain, grow and advance. Eventually, all other art forms evolve into businesses. Music, design, fashion, photography, theater, and film are "industries." Business has brought a level of innovation and creativity to these art forms and how they, in turn, are used to conduct and promote business.

Viewing business as art helps us understand how it became the source of so much innovation, creativity, and influence. This approach also helps us understand and what motivates us, the ways we participate in business, and the roles we undertake, such as customer and consumer, advocate and marketer, inventor and designer, customer service representative, marketer, salesperson, process and systems creator, and financial manger. Finally, of course, there is the role of leader.

A great place to start unraveling the question of why we participate in business is to explore our motivation. The answer is simple. It is the force of human emotion, which results from our desires and how we feel about meeting them. When our needs are met, we feel content and behave in a way that will further that happiness.

When our needs are not met, we feel angry, upset, or disappointed. As a result, we're likely to behave in a manner we think will get us what we want. This can include withdrawing, looking for sympathy, blaming others, arguing, or threatening. All are aimed at overcoming our anger or disappointment and influencing others to meet our desires.

BACON AND EGGS ANYONE?

Review the following list of twelve of the most influential businesspeople in recent history. Is there any name you're not familiar with?

- Bill Gates
- Oprah Winfrey
- John D. Rockefeller
- Henry Ford
- Mark Zuckerberg
- Walt Disney
- Coco Chanel
- Thomas Edison
- Warren Buffet
- Edward Bernays
- Steve Jobs
- J.P. Morgan

The odds are fairly good that Edward Bernays is the only unfamiliar name. Who is he, and why is he included? The answer tells us something about how marketing and advertising reached such a sophisticated level of influence.

The idea that we purchase products to fulfill our desires and that our buying decisions are based on emotions rather than logic is certainly not new. While several versions of how this evolved exist, they all involve Bernays, an Austrian-born immigrant to America, who is considered one of the most influential minds of the last century. Bernays, who is known as "the father of public relations" and "the father of spin," pioneered public relations. He provided the foundation for emotional selling and marketing and influenced much of the twentieth-century's economic and political thought. In the mid-1920s, the Beech-Nut Packing Company saw its revenue from bacon sales lagging and turned to Bernays for help. Before Bernays, the assumption was that people used logic to make decisions. Bernays, however, was influenced by his uncle Sigmund Freud, who believed that people are more motivated by emotion.

Thus, Bernays understood that much of human behavior is driven by instinct and unconscious desires. As a result, he believed that appealing to the public's emotions would result in greater sales than promoting the dependability and reliability of a product. Thus, to sell more bacon, Bernays decided to create an emotional appeal for a heartier breakfast that included bacon. In the mid-1920s, the ideal American breakfast was toast, juice, and coffee. To change people's thinking, he asked over 4,500 physicians whether they thought a "light" or a "hearty" breakfast was healthiest. The physicians overwhelmingly chose the hearty breakfast.

Bernays' idea of a hearty breakfast included bacon and eggs, so he used this definition when he released the findings of his study. The news made headlines. Within a short time, bacon and eggs became America's breakfast. Beech-Nut Packing enjoyed a significant increase in bacon sales, and breakfast was redefined. Bacon and eggs, or some variation remains, by far, America's best-selling breakfast. This includes McDonald's McMuffin.

Bernays' contribution remains incredibly powerful. The idea that what we buy is driven by emotion is how products or services are marketed, branded, and sold today. Automobiles sales play on motivating the buyer's desire for freedom, luxury, pride, and appearance. Clothing and accessories are marketed to reflect sexual prowess, attractiveness, and status. Food marketers promote physical wellbeing, goodness, and, for "foodies," feeling "in" on the latest trend. Bernays' ideas have been advanced, expanded on, and fine tuned, and emotional selling is still with us. Whenever you hear "doctors recommend" or "more dentists recommend," you have Eddie Bernays to thank.

BACK TO BASICS

At the most fundamental level, the goal of any business is to provide a product or service that responds to and fulfills our needs. It is *why* we engage in business and buy the products or services we do. *What* we buy is the result of our motivation. *How* we do it reflects the process that delivers it to us. To better understand this, we must explore what motivates us to engage one another to fill a need. For example, to fill our need:

- To feel connected and accepted, we engage in communities, which give us a sense of belonging and tribal identity. These communities include religious and civic organizations, clubs, and schools. These are businesses, as are the enterprises, organizations, teams and workgroups, professional associations and affiliations, and the social media we participate in. As we'll explore in Chapter Three, this need is at the core of some of today's most successful products or services.

- For accomplishment and the status that accompanies it, we strive to be successful. Our achievements allow us, and others, to see us as able to reach high levels of performance. We compete to be the best, the smartest, the most knowledgeable, and the most skilled. In business, we compete with one another in the hierarchies that are part of our workgroups, teams, and organizations. We demonstrate the rewards through the products or services we buy and the social merit we contribute.

- For self-actualization, we engage in personal development and growth, such as the study of spirituality, religion, and self-awareness, to be in harmony with the world, to be at peace with ourselves and others, and to find self-acceptance and love. We may also be customers of businesses that provide opportunities for self-discovery, personal growth, and power, and that assist us in our pursuit of abundance.

- To be conscious of our environment, we engage in practices that are ecofriendly. We choose goods and services that lessen our footprint and restore what we've taken from the earth. We create technologies and products that diminish the impact of pollution and, in some cases, eliminate the loss of natural resources. From the upstream biofriendly and safe products to the downstream providers of recycling services, we participate in protecting and improving the planet.

- To be helpful and compassionate, we engage in activities and contribute money and other resources to causes that alleviate hunger and poverty and help others in times of crisis.

These examples provide insight into human nature and what motivates us to participate in business as we do.

Our understanding and ability to apply the elements of the Business Code helps us interpret why we buy what we buy and how we do it. The more a product or service fulfills a need, the more we are attracted to it. The greater our attraction is, the stronger the offering. The stronger the offering, the more powerful the brand. The more powerful the brand, the more value the product or service has.

WE LIKE WINNING

I often ask audiences, "Why are you in business? What is it you're trying to do?" The most frequent and confident response is, "To make money!"

That's not a wrong answer. There's a great deal of truth in it. After all, one of the measures of business success is profit. Profit is part of the end-game; the scorecard. Making money is the measuring stick of capitalism.

In my view, the purpose of a business, regardless of the product or service and whether it's a for-profit or not-for-profit enterprise, is to win the customer. That's what business is all about.

I then ask, "What do you offer the customer that allows you to be successful and make money?" Answers include:

- "Superior customer service!"
- "Added value!"
- "A product our customer can depend on!"
- "We give them quality!"
- "I offer them something they can't get anywhere else!"
- "We provide expertise!"
- "A wide selection of options and choices!"
- "We give our customers peace of mind!"
- "To bring value to people's lives!"
- "We provide solutions!"
- "Helping our customers reach their goals!"

It's interesting when members of the same team give different answers. If there's going to be misalignment among members of a group and a conflict over who is right and who is wrong, this is where it starts.

Winning the customer is the result of delivering a product or service in a way that motivates the customer to buy it. They choose to spend their money on your offering rather than on someone else's—your competitor. Competition is a key driver and motivator of business. The foundation of our capitalist system is our shared desire to compete. The winners reap the benefits, so it is natural that we compete to win.

When a customer pays enough for your product or service to make a profit, you can invest that profit to increase your ability to win and build your business to win even more.

Winning isn't our only motivation; several others contribute to our propensity to participate, including the social benefit we create and deliver.

A powerful aspect of an organization's alignment resides in *what* is being created and delivered. Behind every product or service there is a purpose—a reason *why* the product or service has value. Finally, there is *how* the product is created and delivered to the customer. These three are the centerpiece for what it takes to win in business, and together they provide the foundation for how the four elements of the Business Code come together.

In the next chapter, we'll explore how these forces influence the cultures of our teams and organizations, engage us in our leadership preferences, and result in the consistent thinking and behavior business demands.

TWO

The Business Code

At the heart of complexity lives simplicity.

Aligning a business, company, or team requires a clear and constant focus, continuous effort, and all the skills necessary to be a great leader today and tomorrow. Members of organizations and teams must be more engaged and committed than ever before. For this, they need as much information and development as their leaders do. Every member of every team or company has a role in ensuring that alignment exists.

Business has become ever more complex as the speed of change increases. Too often, we remain committed to old ideas and methods embedded in the last century's management thinking. The degree to which we've internally focused on the creation and maintenance of often-disconnected processes and systems adds to the misalignment of companies or teams.

The future seems increasingly unpredictable. Our sense of safety has eroded, and our expectations for stability are harder to fulfill. The promises of the past are vague remnants of motivations that are no longer credible and carry little influence in today's workplace. Many shifts in the workforce turned out to be greater than most people expected, thereby creating uncertainty.

Four generations are now part of an increasingly diverse workforce; they have differing perspectives and expectations. The global marketplace, once confined to geographic delineation, is melding and shifting.

With it, a global workforce demands mobility and opportunity. The changing face of society is only outpaced by the changing face and increasing turnover in personnel.

Bookstores and the Internet offer endless products and streams of business ideas and approaches to leadership. The varieties and choices available for strategic implementation are mind boggling. If you add the availability of technology, information, and the speed of communication, it's easy to understand that the level of focus and commitment required to create and lead alignment can be overwhelming.

To confront this challenge, leaders need a systemic framework for understanding, assessing, and creating alignment. They and their teams and organizations require an approach that cuts through the complexity and eliminates the noise from multiple priorities, numerous initiatives, and the confusion of choices and options; an approach that provides a clear and simple roadmap to success.

The Business Code starts simply, letting us discover the richness of how business fulfills our needs. It allows us to connect the needs of the customer to our brand's intention as delivered through the products or services provided. Next, it connects the ways in which we lead and operate our businesses and shows how they can be aligned to become more effective and efficient.

There are four elements to this systemic approach: *the customer, brand intention, culture* and *leadership* (see Figure 2.1). The framework provides a measurable and observable means of articulating and aligning company culture to customer expectations. This particular alignment presents a significant challenge. For most leaders, their organization or team's culture is defined through values and beliefs, and then further interpreted by the individual. In meeting this challenge, the Business Code provides a comprehensive lens through which to view the patterns of behavior by which culture can be intentionally led. It provides a systemic approach to aligning internal behavior—how a company or team's members engage each other—to external behavior—how they engage the customer.

When the four elements of the Business Code are aligned, the result is *the beauty of business*. We can observe it and describe it intellectually. We can experience it and feel it emotionally. We can also see and feel when it is not present. When the components are aligned, the customer

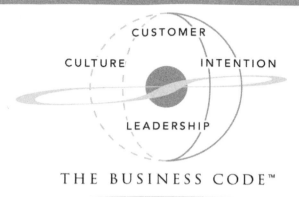

Figure 2.1 The Business Code

experiences satisfaction and trust. When there is misalignment, the customer experiences disappointment, anger, resentment, and mistrust. Similarly, the same experiences are apparent in teams and organizations, and inevitably influence the customer experience.

THE CUSTOMER

Jan Moore, an entrepreneur and good friend says, "Nothing happens until someone sells something. And nothing is sold until you have a customer to sell it to." Jan's assessment has stood the test of time. Without customers, there is no business. Therefore, the first element of the Business Code is the *customer*.

A customer can be defined narrowly or broadly. Narrowly, *a customer is the person who pays for your product or service*. Broadly, *a customer is any person who buys and receives or is affected by your product or service*. Whichever definition you choose, a business requires customers— at least one. Too often, companies fail to clearly articulate and communicate who their customer is and what is at the center of that relationship.

One aspect of either description that is evident and doesn't change is that customers are people. In consumer markets that's obvious. In business-to-business markets and transactions, where the customer is another company or business, it's important to remember that the buying decisions are still made by people, whether it's one person or a group of people. In business-to-business selling, it is important to know who the decision makers are.

All customers make decisions based on a combination of logic and emotion. While we have an incredible ability to think logically, we act out of emotion. Beneath the surface are human desires, the root causes that motivate our actions. Understanding how these motivations affect a customer's decision to buy a particular product or service is at the core of creating customer satisfaction.

For example, a customer buying a car has many options. He may visit dealerships in search of the car of his dreams—a BMW or an Audi sports sedan or convertible. He not only wants to feel that he is accomplished enough to afford such a car—including the higher insurance rates and maintenance costs—he also wants to look and feel as if he can drive a car capable of fast acceleration. Emotionally, it's an important part of the image he wishes to present. He wants to test drive the available models to make sure they have an impressive sound system, the color is just right, and that he looks good in it. He expects to pay more to get what he wants, even if he has to order and wait for it. He has enough of a down payment to get into the car, yet is also considering a lease. He may be willing to make some compromises to get the car more quickly, yet is mindful not to let the allure of immediate gratification get in the way of getting it just right.

Another car shopper goes online and, rather than look for the car of his dreams, looks for something reliable at the best price. He visits sites that offer efficiency and effectiveness and allow him to make the fastest, most accurate comparisons. Relative to what he is willing to spend, he has a sizeable down payment and plans to pay the loan off as quickly as he can. While color and sound system may be considerations, they are not deal breakers. He is looking for the best price on a low-cost-of-ownership vehicle with high fuel efficiency and looks for an apples-to-apples comparison. He may be willing to make some compromises to get a car more quickly, yet getting the lowest price is foremost.

Both customers want to be satisfied with their choice. Each has clear criteria by which they define success. Each considers price and wants to get the most for his money. Yet their perspectives on what they're willing to spend and the value associated with it differ. One wants to look and feel good about being able to afford the car; the other wants to feel that he made the best choice of a car that fits his price. They take different routes to shopping and buying and have different approaches to how they will interact with the provider of their prospective cars. Each takes on similar yet different decisions, and each wants to feel satisfied with his experience. They may have similar ideas about what good customer service is, yet they have different expectations about the level of attention or knowledge they will receive from the seller. While they both may seek financing, they likely have different requirements.

Both customers are buying cars. We can readily see how they are alike. Relative to the particular car, each is shopping for a good deal and looking to get the most for his money. Each has requirements and criteria on which to base his decision. They are both motivated to shop and buy.

We can also see how they are different: They have different tastes, dissimilar styles, conflicting perspectives on value, and divergent buying habits. While they are both motivated, they are differently motivated. If we look more closely at each customer, we will likely find that the sources of their motivation, the desire each is fulfilling through the purchase of a car, are different.

In business, nothing is more important than understanding customer motivation. Although you may begin creating a new product or service without interfacing with a customer, you eventually find yourself seeing the customer at the core of your business. Even if you're like Steve Jobs, who believed that Apple would lead the customer, you still rely on customers for your success. The difference is how you go about it.

To know what the customer wants and how to deliver it, you have to understand what motivates their behavior. To know this, just look at yourself. We are all customers and are motivated by a basic set of needs. This is why you were able to identify with the two car buyers.

In the next chapter, we will explore what these motivations are and how to use them to better understand who customers are, why they act the way they do, and how to please them best. Alignment starts with the customer.

BRAND INTENTION

This next element of the Business Code depends on the first and is leveraged by our understanding of what motivates the customer. I call it *brand intention. Brand intention is the thoughtful and deliberate delivery, through a product or service, of a promise to the customer.*

Over the last several decades, we've devised many ways to define a brand, including market differentiator, value proposition, competitive advantage, mission, purpose, and value-add. Although brands were developed as symbols to distinguish one cattle owner's livestock from another's, it's used in business as a means to differentiate one provider's product or service through a name, trademark, or logo.

Brand statements typically represent promises and offers. How we receive them differs from how we experience intention. Promises are statements that are made. *Intention is how the specific purpose is delivered.* Intention is your perception of how well I deliver on my promise. It is the outcome of thoughtful and deliberate behavior.

Beyond a statement of promise, brand intention goes further. It answers the question, "Why is the customer spending their money with us and not our competitor?" It speaks not just to the promise; it also captures how customers experience the way the promise is delivered and their resulting level of trust. From a customer's perspective, *brand intention reflects the quality of purposefulness through which the product or service is delivered.*

Brand intention is so powerful because it fulfills a customer's desires and motivation. This is an important aspect of alignment. The brand intention tells the customer, at a conscious or subconscious level, that the need they are seeking to fill will be met. As we'll further explore in Chapter Four, each of the six distinct brand intentions connects to and delivers in response to an aspect of motivation. When an organization or team is aligned with its brand intention—to the promise and how it is delivered—the customer experiences it on an emotional level. This makes it a powerful source of competitive advantage.

CULTURE

The third element of the Business Code is culture, which for several very good reasons often presents some of the most challenging aspects of alignment. First, most leaders and the members of their teams and organizations struggle to define their culture. Second, most leaders are not trained or given the knowledge and skills to lead a culture effectively. As a result, they are left to teach themselves. Thus, most of their ability, in this critical aspect of leadership, is the result of trial and error.

Third, leaders tend to define their cultures by communicating its values and beliefs. While this is important, it's rarely articulated in a way that creates an understanding of how things should be done. This causes confusion and conflict over issues of role definition, power and influence, compensation and reward, decision-making, and the management of disagreements.

Culture defines how people treat one another, including the patterns and norms of behavior that members engage in at an individual and group level to achieve success. Culture defines acceptable and unacceptable behavior. When we talk about getting the right people on to the bus, culture describes what the bus looks like and how the people on it are expected to act. One aspect of great businesses is the alignment of internal behaviors to the external experience of the customer, and culture is the key influencer of how the customer is treated. When this alignment occurs, it creates incredible power.

This is the power conveyed by the alignment of Apple's culture to the experience of a customer visiting one of its over 400 worldwide retail locations. Apple places enormous emphasis on the expertise and competencies of its employees. Apple's culture emphasizes its capability to innovate and the degree to which its employees are expected to show their passion and expertise in everything they do. The company claims to be amazing and requires its retail sales employees to be analytical, tech savvy, and insightful. It demands that they learn, develop and inspire–that they be amazing.

These expectations are not lost on the customer. From the moment you walk into an Apple store, an employee, acting as an expert guide, asks why you are there and connects you with the person who has the knowledge to best help you. Behind each employee is a learning and development plan that is reviewed vigorously and which the employee must achieve to meet the expectations of the culture. The benefit results from advancing the employee's expertise and providing a positive customer experience. This is alignment. It is rare that the employee engaging a customer does not know how to answer the question or solve the problem, yet if they can't, they'll quickly connect you with someone who can.

A key aspect of the alignment of culture to brand intention and the customer is that how members of an organization or team behave toward one another is how the customer is treated. As an Apple employee, learning and developing is expected, and managers and employees are continuously engaged in that process. It is aligned to the approach they take with their customers. If an employee is not committed to this endeavor and is not willing to continuously learn and improve, they are not a good fit. Expertise and passion are requirements that are a part of the definition of the employee experience. They are also required aspects of the customer experience.

How learning and development is used within a culture is only one of many levers that influence the alignment of a culture and the experience of the customer. Chapter Eight provides other measurable and observable characteristics that will you help you better identify what is and is not aligned in your culture. It will also provide you with a set of strategies to better align your culture to your customer's expectations, increase your likelihood of success and your organization or team's performance results.

LEADERSHIP

The fourth element of the Business Code is *leadership*. Among a leader's many responsibilities, none is as powerful and integral to success as understanding culture. Therefore, the leader's behavior must be in alignment with the culture's expectations. Without this, it is virtually impossible to create and lead an aligned organization or team. As complex as the study of leadership is, the most straightforward definition of leadership is *influencing others to act*. Leaders are responsible for acting in a manner that clearly conveys how the intention of the business is implemented and ultimately how the customer is treated.

To influence culture, leaders primarily do three things. They role model acceptable behaviors, which define how individual and group success are achieved; they reinforce what is acceptable and unacceptable behavior; and they represent the reputation of the culture. As we'll explore in Chapter Ten, these basic aspects of aligned leadership are not to be taken lightly. The influence a leader has, formally and informally, can easily be undermined when a leader's behavior is misaligned.

Another aspect of a leader's influence that is often overlooked is how well aligned the leader's natural preference is to the strategies the group is undertaking. The way we behave comes from our psychological makeup and preferences. How we are wired directly impacts how we think strategically, as well as how we relate to the customer experience. This preference guides our beliefs about what, why, and how a product or service is offered and delivered to the customer.

The customer ultimately experiences the preferences of the leader. You don't have to look hard to find examples. Just consider Henry Ford, Oprah Winfrey, Bill Gates, Indra Nooyi, Richard Branson, Steve Jobs, Warren Buffet, Steve Wynn, Walt Disney, and Mark Zuckerberg. Each demonstrates their personal preference in how they lead, as well as the market strategies and brand intentions they pursue. For example, Howard Schultz, the CEO of Starbucks, believes that connecting to and caring for people is paramount to success. This not only extends to the strategies for how Starbucks engages its customers; it is also evident in the company's human resource strategies.

Schultz was born and raised in the Bronx, New York, where his family lived in a housing project. He often refers to his father, who struggled in low-paying jobs and had little money, no health insurance, and no workers' compensation insurance when he got hurt on the job. In Starbucks, Schultz set out to build a company in which employees would be respected and well cared for. While the company's main goal was to serve a great cup of coffee and to connect and care for its customers, Schultz said he wanted to build a "company with a soul."

Schultz's values and preferences resulted in a set of practices that are uncommon in retail businesses. Employees working at least 20 hours per week receive comprehensive health coverage for themselves and their families, as do unmarried couples. Along with stock option plans, employees are given a great deal of personal responsibility and treated with the respect that Schultz thought his father deserved and hadn't received. How employees are treated by supervisors and the benefits they receive result in high loyalty and lower turnover.

These innovations come from Schultz's life experience and personal preferences. They are evident in the company's strategies, including, in the early stages of the company's growth, never to franchise. This decision avoided any possible dilution of, or variations in, the company's culture and assured consistency in how both customers and employees are treated. In the case of Schultz and Starbucks, the alignment of a leader to the company's market strategy and culture is apparent. The influence of his leadership on the organization's performance is difficult to debate, and his reputation as a leader is undeniable. In 2011, he was named *Fortune Magazine*'s Businessperson of the Year.

Aligned leadership is a key aspect of business success regardless of size. In a smaller company, the influence of the leader is more obvious and more easily observed and recognized. Just think about a small family business or partnership that employs only two or three people. Customers directly feel and experience the leader's influence in how they are treated and, subsequently, tie it to how the business and its leader are described.

As a company grows, the alignment of leadership becomes more challenging because different people in a variety of leadership positions bring their own perspectives, experiences, and personalities into the mix. Together, they have as great a role in consistently influencing everything from the customer experience to strategic implementation and the effects of role modeling and reinforcement of a company's culture as does the leader of a smaller business. Just as Howard Schultz sees the world through the lens of his experiences and preferences, so do the numerous leaders in a company the size of Starbucks.

Developing and teaching leaders how to lead in an aligned fashion and to act and make decisions aligned to the company's vision, strategy, and goals is one of the keys to success. After all, all eyes are on the leader, an aspect of leadership that can never be overlooked. It's not always about what a leader says, which undoubtedly is of great importance, it's about what a leader does.

Leadership is the fourth element of the Business Code. When joined with the elements of the customer, brand intention, and culture, leaders have incredible influence and often hold the key to alignment. As we'll explore in the next several chapters, a common thread that runs through the four elements of the Business Code is the shared human experience rooted in our motivations, emotions, and needs. While none of the four elements work without the others, teams and companies require aligned leadership to attain the highest levels of performance and success.

When the four elements of the Business Code come together, the power they create results in extraordinary performance.

THREE

The Customer

To know our customer is to know our business.

What separates market leaders from their competitors? What makes your product or service different from the rest? Although a number of factors are important, the one that matters most is the answer to, "Why is the customer spending money with us rather than with our competitors?"

At the center of every great market strategy is the ability to clearly communicate and then consistently deliver what the customer is paying for regardless of the product or service, regardless of market complexity or size. This is what motivates the customer. It is the difference between those companies that become market leaders and those that struggle to get and sustain customer attention. Whether competing in a small local market or on the global stage, such clarity and relentless pursuit of customers results in successful brand identities. They are the household names and trusted brands of the most sought after products or services. Often, they assume legendary status.

Brand clarity and what it represents to customers are key to any business's success. However, this is where companies often fall short and is the core reason why customers are *not* attracted to a particular product or service. A lack of clarity also has an impact on employees, who are expected to successfully meet customer needs. It can also cause confusion and misalignment within organizations, creating unnecessary and unproductive conflict that inevitably erects barriers to performance. This results in imprecisely defined and interdependent strategies and goals, finger pointing for performance failures, and a lack of commitment and accountability. It's hard to create success when we're not clear and aligned on what we're selling to the customer.

To appreciate the extraordinary power of brand intention, we must understand more about *why* and *how* we buy *what* is being offered. The *what* and the *how* are factored into the customer's perception of the intention of the provider, yet neither would be necessary without first understanding *why* people buy.

In today's ongoing battle to provide more and more to the customer and to increase value, products and services have grown enormously complex. Have you ever asked yourself "What am I really buying?" You probably have and can relate to the confusion.

In the blur of rapid improvements and accelerated changes, customers can quickly be confused by the number of options. Often, customers define success as the ability to select and buy more easily—to readily identify what they are looking for, to experience fewer complications, and actually get what they're paying for.

CUSTOMER MOTIVATION

To understand how a customer determines the true value of a product or service is to understand why we are motivated to buy a product or service in the first place. The answer is simple—and powerful—we *buy products or services to fulfill our human wants and needs*; that is, to make ourselves feel good. This most basic of human motivations lies at the core of consumerism, including business-to-business transactions.

For most of the twentieth century, we described customer purchasing as a three-legged stool, meaning that they bought based on three values: quality, service, and price. Conventional thinking was that you could offer the customer "two-out-of–three." "You can't have all three," the customer was told.

Then, in the decades between 1970 and 2000, market leadership began to require a different approach. Popular research demonstrated that to gain and hold true market leadership, companies and organizations had to master one of three strategic approaches: customer relationship and synergy, quality and product leadership, or low cost. In *Discipline of Market Leaders*, Michael Treacy and Fred Wiersema contended that to win or claim market leadership, organizations needed to be expert at one of these core approaches. They had to be good at the other two, and mastery of one was essential.

Unfortunately, most businesses confused operational excellence with low price. By low cost, the authors meant increasing efficiencies and lowering the expenses associated with the creation and delivery of a product or service to the customer; this is not the same as low price. As we'll explore in Chapter Five, differentiating between the two and how they are applied strategically is critical. Not doing so can lead to significant internal misalignment and confuse customers. The customer is often willing to pay more for a product, even when little cost is associated with its creation, production and delivery. Low cost does not always lead to low price.

Along with customer relationship and synergy, quality and product leadership, and low cost, another customer value proposition is often overlooked. It is the feeling of fulfillment we get from helping others as well as caring for ourselves. The desire to improve our health, physical environment, and psychological well-being is at the core of many buying decisions and helps explain why people are willing to give money to not-for-profits, even though they do not directly receive a product or service in return. It also explains why we purchase products or services that fulfill the need to take care of ourselves and others.

The idea that we buy products to feel good links well with the idea of emotional selling. The more we understood about "why" people buy, the more creative and sophisticated we became at innovating and creating products or services to satisfy human need and the more sophisticated and refined we became in selling them. This ability to innovate, create, and refine continues to grow.

In Chapter One, I introduced you to the influence of Edward Bernays, and the simple and powerful idea behind emotional selling. To do this successfully, you have to understand how to decode the customer and identify the source of his or her motivation.

Decoding the customer provides a framework for understanding why we are attracted to and buy products or services; it offers a means through which we can better define customer motivation. It provides a foundation from which we can better leverage our ability to brand, market, and sell more effectively. Success is rooted in understanding what motivates us. It connects the intuitive sense of why we buy what we buy to the deep psychological motivators of our behavior and offers a framework for connecting human desire to strategic intention, brand marketing, and selling strategies. It helps us understand and articulate our competitive differentiator.

Beginning in the late the 1950s, Will Schutz presented a very powerful and simple explanation of human behavior and interaction known as FIRO (Fundamental Interpersonal Relations Orientation) theory. Schutz's work is remarkable because we can take almost any other model for understanding human behavior and connect it to his findings and insights.

In 1952, Schutz , a research psychologist, was asked by the U.S. Navy to determine how teams of men could better work together to make better decisions, thereby improving team performance, particularly under pressure. Schutz theorized that all of our behavior and interaction is motivated by three fundamental desires to feel (1) important; (2) competent; and (3) accepted.

What Schutz probably didn't see was that the profound understanding of human behavior he developed would provide a powerful framework for understanding why customers buy what they do in the way they do, what they are seeking for themselves and their individual sense of fulfillment, and how products or services are offered.

This may seem overly simple, yet you will soon recognize it everywhere—in every product or service you already own and use and in those you are considering for future purchase.

Schutz's FIRO theory can also be used to better understand the what, why, and how of branding, marketing, selling, and product or service delivery. It allows us to interpret why customers react to products or services with a range of responses from euphoria and joy to disappointment, anger and despair. It's all about whether customers feel fulfilled by what they purchased.

As customers, the three sources of human motivation are consistent with how we react in other situations. It's easy to underestimate the value of a customer's experience and the power of our desires. When our needs are met, we typically feel good. When they are not met, we quickly be-

Figure 3.1 The Three Customer Motivations

come disappointed and angry. As marketers, we should try never to overlook the human component of what makes the customer experience so powerful. We should try to always consider what motivates us as customers and respond to the three motivations that we all share. In no order of importance, customers want: *attention, competency,* and *caring* (Figure 3.1).

Attention

Attention fulfills our need to feel important and supports our desire to know that we count. The opposite is to feel ignored, which customers interpret as they don't matter and are not valued. This is a powerful force and, as with most emotional responses, is immediate. Think about the last time you called for customer service and went through several telephone prompts before you got a person on the phone. Like me, you probably tried to outsmart the recording by saying "customer rep," "agent," "customer service," or by pressing "0," "9," or "1," only to find yourself back at the main menu.

It doesn't take much for this to make us anxious, upset, or angry. It's hard for even the greatest of brands and businesses to recover from ignoring the customer.

In our relationships to one another, the first indicator of mutual respect is whether one person shows an interest in the other. I define mutual respect as people treating one another in the manner in which they want to be treated. This is not possible unless each person is willing to pay attention and listen to the other. The focus on attention is the key to the brand strength of Lands' End and defines its customer service. Until the latter part of 2012, when it first incorporated a voice prompt system, customer calls were answered at any time of the day or night within two rings. Twenty-four hours a day, seven days a week, you found yourself talking to real person, not an automated system of multiple menus. The speed with which the company connected by telephone and now online chat is vital to how its customers interpret the value of its products. This focus on customer attention is Lands' End's passion and shows up in every facet of the organization. Many businesses can sell you a quality shirt. It is how Lands' End does it that makes the difference. By paying attention and thereby making the customer feel important, Lands' End separates itself from its competition.

Many powerful and successful brands now motivate customers by paying attention to them. Think about Facebook, YouTube, and the host of providers of social media. Being "social" is engaging in giving and receiving attention from one another. In light of our current demographics, this is a powerful force. Whether a business is large or small, demographics should not be overlooked when defining brand strategy.

As we move through the second decade of the twenty-first century, , the baby boomer generation is the largest group in our economy and workforce. In the United States, there are 76 to 80 million people in this generation.

The second largest group is the Echo or Millennium generation, also known as Generation Y or the New Millennials—the children of the baby boomers. Born between the early 1980s and the early 2000s, this group is 72 to 75 million (U.S.) strong. Its members grew up with the new technology and has come to rely on it, spending endless amounts of time using it. Depending on the study, sociologists claim that 35 to 45 percent of the formative years of New Millennials were spent alone in front of computer screens, televisions, and video games. As a result, they crave attention. As they moved through adolescence and entered adulthood as consumers, this need became a major influence—one well worth business leaders' attention (no pun intended).

The generation immediately before them, Generation X, includes approximately 49 to 51 million (U.S.) people born between the mid 1960s and early 1980s. This is a much smaller group. Often referred to as the ignored generation, when it comes to technology and need for attention, this group shares many of the characteristics of the GenYers.

In addition to explaining why social media has become such a global force and phenomenal marketing tool, the demographic data demonstrates how powerful attention is to businesses. There's a significant benefit to understanding its part in the emotional attractiveness of a product or service and how it can be leveraged through a company's product or service and brand intention.

Attention is a key to building successful customer relationships and is the cornerstone and foundation for many great brands and the intention of their products or services. Its importance is not limited to large businesses. Like Disney, Harley-Davidson, and Lands' End, even the smallest business can leverage attention as a key value and source of motivation.

Competency

We expect providers of products or services to be competent both in creating and delivering whatever it is we're buying. Beginning with the design and engineering that goes into a product and continuing with how it is delivered, we expect a level of reliability and quality that reflects the provider's competency. From the person making the sale to the delivery person handing us the product to the person on the phone (or online) helping fix a problem, we expect competency. If we purchase using an automated or technology-based process, such as a website or telephone-based system, we expect that system to be designed in a customer-oriented and competent manner, allowing us to be successful.

A customer's trust in the provider's competency and the quality of a product or service is a direct reflection of the customer's competency in making the decision to buy a particular product or service. When customers make a good decision, they feel competent and conclude that they made the right choice. When customers feel they made a bad choice or decision, they feel incompetent and experience the anxiety that accompanies the embarrassment of making the wrong choice. The customer may even feel stupid, which is not a good outcome for anyone.

For the customer, status relates to competence. BMW is considered one of the most competent engineering companies in the world. BMW does not sell a car. It sells the "ultimate driving machine." The intention is to communicate that a BMW, through advanced engineering and design and the quality embedded in its manufacture, goes far beyond the expectations of other cars. It is much better than the average car. To the customer, this easily translates to, "I am not your average guy." First, being able to afford a BMW demonstrates the owners' competence. Second, ownership shows they are smart enough to know and drive a great car. Third, they are able to drive such a high-performing machine properly because they are competent drivers. Drivers of BMWs often argue emotionally in support of BMW's quality and craftsmanship and, thus indirectly, in support of their own competency.

When the expected competency is not provided, customers are naturally disappointed and resent the provider for letting them down. We question whether we were incompetent in making the buying decision. We make comparisons about the quality, appearance, and associated pricing because we want to get the best value for our dollar, which makes us feel competent and in control. If we are fooled or make a bad decision, we no longer feel competent. That is why we strive for predictable outcomes.

Every product or service must reach a bar that represents the level of competency that the customer expects. It is a source of trust between the business and its customers and shows up in quality, know-how, expertise, reliability, sound advice, customer service, and durability. All businesses must pay attention to this motivator and always strive to meet that expectation. In order for them to feel competent, customers need to feel secure and trust in your competency. It is often at the center of why they are choosing to spend their money with you.

Caring

We all want to feel that whomever we are buying from is treating us well. When we pay for a product or service, we expect to be treated with dignity and respect and to receive what the provider promised. This begins with how well the provider markets what it is selling and how transparent and honest the company is in the message provided in its advertising. Caring conveys that you'll be truthful with me.

We have become accustomed to accepting less than we bargained for. We know that the advertising is not always accurate and more often tests the boundaries of truth and reality. Still, we expect that the makers and deliverers of the products or services we want will inevitably do the right thing and deliver on their promise.

The expectation of being treated in a caring way often extends beyond the immediate locus of the customer to the communities, the environment, and other relationships. While truth in advertising is one example, social responsibility, fair trade, and societal benefit are examples of how caring is experienced in broader ways. Along with a customer's singular experience, the failure to create a shared value is interpreted by customers as a lack of caring about them and their world. Often, this is measured by how truthful the product or service provider is; how what they do is measured in terms of what is ethical and "right."

The motivation behind caring is the customer's desire to feel affection and acceptance. In addition to the sense of caring conveyed by honesty and openness, the customer can experience physical and emotional well-being, as well as a fulfillment of the ongoing desire for self-actualization, through products or services. Thus, when we buy a product or service that delivers caring, we also care for ourselves. This means pursuing and becoming who we want to be physically and emotionally and learning what makes us happy about who we are. These desires show up in our appearance, our physical health, our energy, and so on. We want to be cared for, care for ourselves, and care for others.

Whole Foods, the world's largest retailer of natural and organic foods, has done a remarkable job of focusing on the customer motivation of caring. The idea of good food for good people and a good earth underlines the caring quality of the company and how it achives this goal. This experience is a key to the customer's motivation. The emotional value is so great that the customer is willing to pay more for it. In paying more for caring, the consumers underlying expectation is to be treated in alignment to that intention. Another aspect of the Whole Foods approach focuses on its authenticity and honesty in customer relations. There is a powerful element embedded in the idea that Whole Foods is in competition with the big grocery food chains that do not care enough about their customers.

As we will explore in Chapter Five, caring is also evident in the products or services customers engage in as part of their lifelong journey of self-actualization. The result is self-discovery and self-acceptance. Often, such products or services offer philosophical approaches to life, ideas for living, and processes that customers use to reach their goals. As a result, the provider can often enjoy high profit margins. People are willing to pay to care for themselves.

What separates market leaders from their competitors is the ability to deliver through their product or service a uniqueness that differentiates them from the rest. To accomplish this means answering the question, "Why is the customer spending money with us rather than our competitors?" The three customer motivations help us understand the sources of a customer's emotional desire to buy and offer insight into what separates the winners from their competitors.

FOUR

Brand Intention

A brand without trust is a name without value.

Myriad factors separate market leaders from their competition, yet the one that matters most is the reason why their customers chose them. Whether in a business-to-consumer or business-to-business relationship, customer motivation is key to understanding how and why customers buy. It is also at the core of the definition of *brand intention*.

A business's mission, purpose, or passion can be described in many ways, yet brand intention goes further in defining the actual customer experience. It applies the concepts of market differentiation, competitive advantage, and value proposition and applies to the actual customer experience. Each of these makes promise that customers can easily identify with and understand. When your actions reflect the promise, customers come to trust it. This is how customers experience your true intention. Trust is all about keeping your promise. *Brand intention goes beyond a statement of promise; it is the thoughtful and deliberate delivery, through a product or service, of your promise.*

It is the moment when the statements of promise manifest as trust in the brand and reinforce the alignment between what is sold and what is bought. By taking actions that actively live up to that promise, you show your true intention. Great brands deliver their brand intention at extraordinary levels. The result is the customer feels he is getting what he paid for. The challenge is to clearly communicate the promise *and* to deliver it in a manner that creates trust.

The same is true of the customer experience. Often, we define customer experience without fully understanding it, which is why companies become misaligned with their customers's expectations. Companies must explore the full scope of that experience to understand how to deliver to it. Saying, "we deliver exceptional customer service," "we provide superior customer satisfaction," or "we meet and exceed our customer's expectations" is not enough. To communicate and align a company's brand intention successfully requires understanding what the customer's intended experience is and aligning everyone's actions, regardless of their role, to achieve it.

THE CUSTOMER EXPERIENCE

We can see the successful delivery of brand intention in virtually every aspect of the customer experience (see Figure 4.1). Responding to the brand intention the customer chooses to spend money on a product or service and the *transaction* takes place. The transaction is the process of buying and receiving the product or service for which the customer is paying. Often, definitions of a transaction focus on the exchange of payment. This is limiting. A transaction is the total customer experience.

Suppose I'm shopping for a new stove. I can do this in one of three ways. I can visit the local appliance dealer. The one near my home is still owned by its founder, who is dedicated to building a family business. His son has grown up in the shop and will eventually take the leadership role from his father. To be competitive, the store offers high-end quality products, expertise, and a promise that, because it is a local family business, there is a greater degree of attention and caring than in the big box stores.

The second option is to visit one or more of the nearby home improvement, hardware, or appliance centers, where I'll have a host of similar brands to choose from, and which are probably not those available from my local dealer—at competitive prices. At the store level, they will likely offer similar levels of expertise and service.

I can also go online and look at various styles, models, and manufacturers, and compare prices. Of course, other considerations will affect my decision-making process, including delivery time, the cost of delivery,

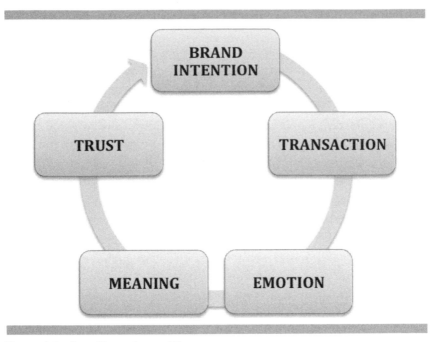

Figure 4.1 Brand Intention and Trust

whether the dealer will connect the stove, the expertise the employees, and how the dealer will dispose of my current unit.

Thus, the transaction has multiple parts. There will be distinct differences in how it will take place depending on where I purchase it and what my expectations are from the various brands. It's not simply choosing a stove and learning the cost. The transaction includes all aspects of my experience: how I am treated by the employees I interact with; the amount of attention I receive; how well I feel employees listened; the level of competency of the salesperson involved (assuming I don't just order online); the timeliness and overall experience of the delivery and installation; the level of openness I experience from the company's representatives; the level of communication, and so on.

A customer typically experiences one of two emotional outcomes from a transaction. The first is satisfaction, resulting in happiness, excitement, joy, contentment, and a general sense of well-being—what is being paid for is being delivered. The second is dissatisfaction, resulting in disappointment, anger, blame, and resentment—not getting what is being paid for.

In reviewing my three options, you might conclude that you get what you pay for. Pay less, and therefore expect less. Pay more, and therefore expect more. When you get what you pay for, you're happy; when you don't, you're angry. It's always about our emotions. *Meaning is the association of our values and beliefs with our experience and emotion.* Meaning is our interpretation of our emotions and helps us understand the reasons behind our feelings. In interactions with people, it is how we describe our intentions toward one another. As customers, we want salespeople to pay attention to us, as this satisfies our need to feel important. We want a product or service competently delivered because it reflects on our competence as a customer; it means I made a great decision. We want to feel cared for and well treated. If you are open and honest with me, it's because you care about me and have nothing to hide.

If I decide to purchase a low-price model to fit my basic needs from a home improvement center, I will have a different experience than if I purchase it from a small store. As I look at the models on display, I expect that eventually someone will ask if I need assistance. As a result, I will have a positive emotional response. The salesperson's attention signals that I am important. If I have to find someone to assist me or if I find the salesperson is unhelpful, I'll feel ignored and frustrated. This will lead to a negative emotional response.

If I ask a salesperson to help me determine the best deal among the lower priced models, and the salesperson helps me find the most stove for my money, I will feel more competent. I will know that I came to the right place and got the best deal. If he is unable to help me, I may feel he is incompetent. In turn, I may feel incompetent for choosing the wrong place. Or, I can blame his incompetence, vent my anger, and convince myself that I did not make a poor choice; the salesperson simply didn't know what he was doing.

What if I tell a salesperson what I'm looking for, and he doesn't listen, steering me toward a higher priced product, all the while sharing how much he knows about it? While I'm not impressed by his listening skills, I may think he's well informed. Yet, because he hasn't responded to my desire, I question whether he is open to my needs or cares about me. If I choose to shop locally, I expect a very knowledgeable salesperson will give me personal attention, will have in-depth knowledge of each product, and will also explore my price range, my cooking habits, and so on to help me find the best stove for my needs. If I decide to buy from him, I expect to receive the same level of expertise and service from the employees who deliver and install it. While I may expect to pay more, the added value—additional attention and caring, as well as the higher level of competency and expertise—might be worth it.

Regardless of the route I take, each option has a set of customer expectations and service criteria connected to it. If my expectations are met, I will be satisfied and happy. If any expectation goes unmet, I will be disappointed. If more than one goes unmet, my negative emotion may escalate and result in feelings of frustration, annoyance, or anger. As customers, the more positive our emotion, the greater our trust. Our interpretation of how well our needs are met gives our experience meaning and is frequently at the center of the story we tell about that experience.

Trust is critical to a mutually beneficial relationship between the provider and the customer. It measures the mutual respect the customer feels when the provider delivers on the promise represented by the product or service and the brand intention. Mutual respect is at the core of that relationship. Trust is the most powerful aspect of brand intention and the key to retaining customers and attracting new ones. It reinforces the value and loyalty associated with a brand and is the major influence over what customers are willing to pay for.

Brand intention defines your promise to your customer. Great brands convey believability and trust and invite the customer to experience what the company is strategically endeavoring to deliver. To do this successfully, a company's market strategy must align with the customer's experience. Since the 1980s, we've relied on a fairly consistent set of similar looking approaches—value proposition, market differentiator, the value-add, and competitive advantage—to interpret and define what the customer wants and then to articulate and connect it to strategy. What started over a century ago as a three-legged stool, representing the three root strategies of quality, service, and price, has evolved into a host of strategies. Low price evolved into the market and organizational strategies of low cost, which resulted in organizational excellence, operational efficiency, and other cost reduction strategies, including those associated with lean manufacturing. Internally, they were aimed at reducing the cost of creating and delivering a product or service to the customer and often supported the goal of winning the customer through competitive pricing.

The art of winning the customer through service matured into more definitive approaches to describing the customer relationship. More advanced service strategies now include the approaches of customer intimacy, customer synergy, and partnering. Over time, quality evolved into such approaches as product or service superiority, uniqueness, and innovation.

Many of these approaches continue to evolve, serve businesses well, and help define what customers buy, yet they often fail to focus on the customer and do not fully recognize or value what a buyer wants. They are often provider focused rather than *customer focused* or *customer centric*. This overall trend is unfortunate. Although these approaches may at times have served business well, they do not provide a complete understanding of what motivates today's customers to buy.

Over the past two decades, the strategic and brand thinking we've relied on has become outdated. A primary reason is the multitude of options offered. Just think of the "better, better, better" and "new and improved" sales pitches that bombard us and the increasing number of options and product features we have to sort through. The overload this creates may leave you questioning the value of what you buy and wishing for simplicity. Psychologically and emotionally, the decisions we feel forced to make are not only confusing they also cause anxiety and stress. They leave us wondering whether we trust that what we get is worth what we're paying for it.

Over time, we've also taken what were once direct marketing and advertising messages and expanded, mixed, and adulterated them to the point where they are no longer connected to the reason why they once worked—human nature. Second, much of the focus on market strategy has been directed inward. In an effort to become more strategic, companies have concentrated more of their efforts on internal processes and systems than on the actual delivery to the customer. Increasing competition and the desire for cost effectiveness has led many companies to pursue goals and objectives that are disconnected from the customer. Furthermore the misalignment of people's day-to-day tasks and activities and the performance goals they support results in a lack of engagement.

One aspect of great strategic thinking that creates higher levels of engagement and success is how well the strategies connect to the what, why, and how a company delivers to its customer. Whether the strategy pertains to product or service development, market development, operational capability, financial management, or human resources, by definition it must support the intentional delivery of the promise made to the customer.

A third reason the long-standing approaches to market strategy are not as effective as they once were can easily be overlooked. It is the confusion that results from thinking that technology, in and of itself, is a brand strategy. Brand loyalty occurs when a person feels an emotional bond to the brand. The human aspect of how a customer experiences the product or service personalizes the brand. The multitude of communication technologies available and the immense power of social media make it more difficult to make these connections.

Social media provide a means to communicate more efficiently with larger numbers of people than ever before, yet a wide reach doesn't typically result in the deep experience that defines our more meaningful connections. Having 1,000 friends on Facebook is not the same as having a few friends with whom you have an intimate and trusting relationship. The same is true of a brand. Unless I am able to consistently convey my intention and deliver it to the customer, my brand has little value no matter how many people know about it.

Companies large and small must continue to evolve their approaches and not rely on past success. The marketplace demands that companies and organizations move forward and think about market strategies and branding in ways that more accurately and powerfully reflect and respond to today's customer. In today's marketplace, winning requires a never-ending dedication to the alignment of a company's brand intention to its customer. In Chapter Five, we'll examine the six brand intentions and how they are evident in many of today's market-leading brands, how they align to the three customer motivations, and how you are affected by them.

FIVE

The Six Brand Intentions

The relentless pursuit of business is winning the customer.

When it comes to the art of business, whether it's the business-to-consumer or business-to-business marketplace, nothing rings more true than the importance of knowing how to win the customer. If you're clear on your brand intention and your company or team is aligned to it, you'll definitely increase your chances to win. Alignment to brand intention is a characteristic and key ingredient that successful market leaders have in common; it plays a significant role in how they beat the competition.

The six brand intentions—*community, customization, preeminence, low price, physical wellbeing, and personal actualization*—provide a framework for understanding and leveraging what the customer is seeking and aligning a company's strategies to meet those expectations. They provide a way to focus on the alignment of what the product or service offers and how a customer need is satisfied. This awareness of what the customer requires for emotional fulfillment is part of the culture of market leaders. They are in tune with what the customer seeks and behave in a manner consistent with those desires. Particularly important is that this awareness is apparent to the customer. This is quite remarkable.

There are certainly other important aspects to how products or services are created and delivered to the marketplace. For example, convenience, speed of delivery, reliability, and availability, none of which should be ignored. They are elements of the customer experience that play a role in and support the brand intention. Indeed, availability and speed of delivery are aspects of how customers define good service and have become givens in our world of fast or instant gratification.

Another force makes the six brand intentions as powerful as they are. It is the fact that they are natural responses to the three customer motivations of attention, competency, and caring. They provide a lens through which to determine which of the three is at the center of the success of a brand and the product or service it represents.

The big take-away from the work of the great thinkers about the art of business is that *the key to success is to identify what the one thing is the customer is buying and to relentlessly pursue its delivery.* In business, although you can be good at many things, strategically you have to be passionate about and master the one thing that you deliver to the market and through which you win the customer. If you look at the research over the past several decades, this has been one of the great guiding principles for creating success. Whether it is a mission statement, purpose, credo, or tagline, the aim is to communicate the brand intention. The clearer and more emotionally grounded the message, the greater the power of the brand.

In the classic comedy film *City Slickers*, Billy Crystal plays Mitch, a middle-aged advertising salesman living in New York City, who is undergoing a midlife crisis. In search of renewal and finding his purpose, Mitch and two of his closest friends go on a cattle-driving vacation. Leading them on the drive is the trail boss Curly, a tough old cowboy who doesn't suffer fools well and who soon finds himself at odds with the three city dwellers. Unexpectedly, Mitch and Curly bond. Mitch confides in Curly and asks him how to confront the issues in his life. Curly advises him to focus on the *one thing* that matters to him most. In business, as in life, it's important to know what the *one thing* is. In today's complex and chaotic world, it's important to know and focus on that one thing. The clearer it is, the more passion we have for it and the more likely we'll live and act in alignment to it. In business, it means aligning every employee and team member to the brand intention. This doesn't mean you should ignore everything else, yet it does mean that everyone understands and acts in alignment to the key deliverable and the supporting priorities of the business.

We often talk about the secret sauces or unique recipes that lead to business success. Over twenty years ago, before becoming a leadership psychologist and student of business, I earned a degree from the Culinary Institute of America, arguably the top cooking school in the world. Along with developing my skills and knowledge and advancing my passion for cooking, a key lesson was that for a customer to consider a dish successful, it has to deliver a tasty and eye-appealing combination of great ingredients. What most customers want is high-quality ingredients combined in a unique and competent manner and priced at a level that reflects the quality and skill with which it is delivered.

This same approach applies to brand intention. The six strategic intentions are not mutually exclusive. Like a great meal, all the ingredients must come together to provide a unique product or service that is creative, innovative, and captures the customer's attention. While the complementary blends and unique combinations are important, ultimately it is the *main ingredient* that must stand on its own and deliver customer satisfaction. If you go to a seafood restaurant and order a fish fillet, it doesn't matter how good the vegetables and potatoes are or how tasty the sauce is. If the fillet isn't as good as advertised, or if it is of lesser quality than the price demands, or it is not prepared correctly, the customer will not be satisfied. The same principle applies to a powerful and successful brand intention. Great products or services, winning brands, and market leaders have this in common. The brand intention is clearly defined, articulated, and delivered. The customer knows clearly what the main ingredient is. This applies as much to business-to-business as it does to business-to-consumer brands.

Another aspect of brand intention that is too often overlooked and undervalued, especially by smaller businesses, is that the more powerful a brand intention is, the more the customer is willing to pay. What the market will bear from a pricing standpoint and the resulting influence on profit margins are almost always related to the clarity and consistency with which the intention is delivered. This kind of brand power and competitive capability should never be underestimated. The only obvious exception is when a brand is engaged in selling on low price. As we'll explore later in this chapter, while I can use five of the six brand intentions to carve out and grow a niche market, low price requires the ability to create volume.

COMMUNITY

Community defines the brand intention of products or services that invite and deliver membership in a group. It offers relationship, affiliation, and connection. *The customer motivation in the brand intention of community is attention.* Community offers a sense of belonging and inclusion. *It satisfies the human need and desire to feel important and have self-worth.* Group members are able to receive attention and give it to others.

Suppose two young, very creative, and intelligent men get together to develop a new product. It began a few years before they met, when a at 21-years old, one began exploring how to bring an idea to fruition. Two years later, he finds someone interested in collaborating with him to create a start-up company and bring the idea to market. They share a vision for what's possible and begin building a prototype in a 10- × 15-foot shed. They work tirelessly and, hoping it will be the beginning of a successful launch into the marketplace, begin seeking people to use their product. Three years later, customers begin to want their product. They find someone willing to sell it for them, develop a logo, move into to a 28- × 80-foot building, and expand their operation to eight people.

The two men continue to recruit talented people interested in collaborating to build the business and, over time, the company grows to over $5 billion in annual revenue. Despite many ups and downs and challenges, they find new ways to collaborate with others, solve problems, and to continue to grow.

The resilience of its brand is defined by how it overcomes great challenges, building an identity of boldness and perseverance. Its customers become some of the most loyal brand ambassadors on the planet and the driving force behind the company's capacity to continually expand and define ways to market and reinvent itself.

The company becomes one of the first to use crowd sourcing to engage its customers to market to others. With little prompting, its customers invite others to join its worldwide following. The company's diverse community, comprised of people in all walks of life and generations, celebrates its shared passion and loyalty for the product and its brand by gathering in groups a half million strong.

Can you correctly select the brand to which this story applies?

1. Nike
2. Harley-Davidson
3. Facebook

4. Geico
5. Budweiser
6. Microsoft

If you chose "b" for Harley-Davidson, you are correct. In 1903, when the company produced its first motorcycles, its inventor William S. Harley was 23 years old and his partner, Arthur Davidson was 22. Their story is familiar in that the company's founders were young, talented, and started the business in a fashion that many of today's success stories mirror. Much like the folklore of the Microsoft garage and the humble beginnings of so many other companies that capture our imaginations, Harley-Davidson started with practically nothing more than a great idea. Over one hundred years later, the company generates over $5 billion in revenue.

At the core of their success is exceptional brand loyalty. The essence of the brand, what makes it so powerful is its incredibly strong brand intention of community. The company's mission statement has community and inclusion embedded in it: "*We* ride *with our customers* and apply *the connection in every market* we serve to create superior value for *all our stakeholders.*"

The company's market strategies embody and continue to be aligned to its brand intention. Much as it did in its early years when it sold to members of the military, the company pursues selling to groups and communities and leveraging camaraderie and affiliation. After World War II, when motorcycle owners loosely grouped into organized clubs, Harley-Davidson captured the idea of community and built its brand around it. Over the years, despite its quality issues, the brand maintained itself by expanding this platform.

Today, the community continues to expand and the company's sales continue to grow. The Sturgis and Daytona motorcycle rallies attract well over a half million riders each. While not directly sponsored by Harley-Davidson, their motorcycles enjoy, by far, the greatest representation at the two events. To further the community brand intention, the company hosts toy drives, conducts cell phones for soldier campaigns, and sponsors concerts and an assortment of other events. It encourages participation in the Harley Owners Group (aka HOG), markets to members of the military, offers group rides, and locally connects individuals to fellow riders. The logo the company unveiled over 100 years ago hasn't changed much, is recognized the world over, and maintains its popularity even as a tattoo, which is a pretty good representation of the power of brand intention.

Another example of the immense power of the brand intention of community and its emotional effects is Facebook. On May 14, 2012, Facebook's IPO was one of the biggest public offerings in history; it raised $16 billion and resulting in a market capitalization of $104 billion for the company. Then its value dropped. Initial trading on the day of the IPO went as high as $38 per share. And, then it fell. By August, shares sold for about $20.

A host of factors affect how people make the decisions to buy and sell stock, and those decisions influence share price. What is so telling about the Facebook IPO is how emotional it was and how much that emotion related to the company's brand intention. The company's founder, Mark Zuckerberg, first created the predecessor to Facebook as a means to connect university students. He soon discovered that people registering for the site wanted to learn more about one another and, more important, wanted others to know about them. Facebook satisfied their human need for attention and connectivity and, along with other social networking services that began emerging, paved the way to leverage technology to accomplish it.

Facebook demonstrates how the human motivation of attention created the emotional influence that led to its IPO value. The emotion associated with the offering was not only about making a quick killing in the market. Underlying the share price was a value associated with the human need for attention, connectivity, and inclusion. At its emotional core, social networking is a way to give and get attention, which satisfies our need to feel important. The more friends I have, the more significant I feel.

Mark Zuckerberg's timing, perhaps inadvertent, was excellent. Today's demographic profile supports the world's rapid adoption of social media. The vast majority of Facebook members are Gen Xers and New

Millennials, who are technology savvy and, based on their life experience, apt to seek social connectivity and the attention that goes with it.

Many companies use the brand intention of community as the engine to deliver their products or services. Disney aspires to inspire *together*, create positive and *inclusive ideas about families*, and provide entertainment experiences *for all generations to share*. Going to Disneyland or Disney World is entering into the Disney community and becoming a member of the worldwide Disney family. Zynga, the company that brings you FarmVille (and soon FarmVille2) has a mission to *connect the world through games*. It is the world's largest provider of social games. The Grateful Dead continues to thrive, adding new generations of fans to its powerful Deadhead nation community.

In business to business, the idea of community has long been established, and exploring its past tells us a great deal about how it can be applied going forward. Trade and professional associations are the hallmarks of community, and they offer it as a value to other businesses and companies. Trade associations target the individual. In business to business, one company attempts to sell its products or services to another, yet, when it comes to selling community, it makes more sense to sell to individuals.

A crossover that demonstrates this principle is the social networking website LinkedIn. The company is the world's largest professional network. At the beginning of 2013, it had over 200 million users worldwide. LinkedIn's success is not in selling business to business. Although it sells advertising to create revenue, it is by engaging individuals—employees of companies large and small—to join its community, that LinkedIn creates its success. It has tapped into the vast rapidly growing market of individual entrepreneurs and single person businesses. Studies show that the trend toward small business includes a growing number of nontraditional workers, including myriad service providers, such as consultants, freelancers, and contractors. It is estimated that by 2015, this group will be 1.3 billion strong worldwide. It should be no surprise that the increase in single-person businesses and companies includes a good percentage of younger people, many of whom want to start their own businesses. What LinkedIn has accomplished through its brand intention demonstrates how valuable community is. For companies and businesses relying on one of the other five brand intentions, community can be a great ingredient in their unique recipe. We already see the trend toward using the term community in lieu of customer base. While every business seeks to grow its community of customers, buyers, and users, that does not mean that it is their brand intention. Using community as an ingredient and marketing strategy in service to the primary brand attraction is different than being the main attraction of your brand and, ultimately, your company.

CUSTOMIZATION

Customization defines the brand intention of products or services to reflect the customer's requirements and wants. It offers a product or service created and delivered to the customer's specifications. *The customer motivation in the brand intention of customization is attention.* Customers know what they want and expect the product or service to be modified, tailored, or made-to-order on their terms. *Customization satisfies the human need and desire to feel important and significant.* As a customer, I own the solution and expect to be heard.

It's not easy to find companies with globally recognized consumer brands or companies of substantial size that provide customization. That doesn't mean they don't exist. Put the word *customized* in front of a product and search on the Internet. In most cases, you'll find a significant set of options. What makes the customization provider unique, and often limits the company's size, is the level of attention required to work with and please the customer.

In business to business, because of the high level of attention required for success, providers of customized products or services often work with a few select customers. These include custom manufacturers, private label products, or prototype manufacturers. Call centers that follow the scripts and processes of the customer and health care contractors that follow the protocols, processes, and procedures of the customer are good examples of customized service providers. The key to success in delivering the brand intention of customization is to pay a high degree of attention to customers and what they want—not to tell them what they need.

As a consumer brand delivering customization, Lands' End has, and continues to, deliver exceptionally well. The company emphasizes, "What is best for the customer is best for the company." The company accepts the return of any item at any time for a full refund of the purchase price or replacement. Lands' End provides replacement buttons or a single glove or mitten should you lose one. The company is committed to making sure you never feel ignored. The employees see themselves as a community and a company dedicated to new ways of connecting and aligning to the idea that the customer is always right. This translates into a high degree of capability to pay attention to the customer and to customize products to the customer's needs.

From big and tall to short and slim for men and petite to plus sizes for women, Lands' End is all about customization and customers getting what they want. When you buy a pair of pants from Lands' End, you can get the waist and leg length tailored to your individual liking. The company will even finish the leg length to within a quarter inch or a half a centimeter and will cuff them in any fashion you like. And, if you don't like the way it fits, even if you're the only person in the world it's made for, you can return it, and the company will issue a full refund.

This relentless pursuit of alignment of brand intention creates extraordinary results in the business-to-business side of the company. Lands' End is expanding globally and wants to become the leading provider of customized corporate wear. Its 2020 vision is to reach $5 billion in revenue and do it in alignment with the customer promise that has become the core of its success. It is an excellent example of how alignment to the brand intention of customization applies to both consumer and business-to-business marketplaces.

When you are a service provider in the business-to-business market, it is important to determine whether you provide a response to the customer's solution or whether you are the solution provider. This is an important distinction that requires clear articulation. The lack of clarity leads to conflict with customers, as well as conflict and misalignment among the parts of a company and members of a team. If the customer gives you the design, solution, or blueprint and expects you to provide it looking exactly as shown, you're delivering customization. Often this also includes specifications and stipulations for how you are to provide, deliver, or implement it. The customer motivation is a high degree of attention and the assurance that they will be listened to and get what they want.

In contrast, if the customer has a problem or need, is unable to create a solution, and looks to you to resolve it, you are selling your competency by providing a solution. This is an important distinction because customer motivation is moving from self-reliance to a dependence on the provider to solve the problem.

A good example is an Australian furniture brand, Evolvex. Providing customized furniture is made more achievable by the software-driven design and manufacturing technology available today. Evolvex has turned over the design to the customer. Options include color, size and configuration. Customers access the design software online and design their own customized desk, table, cabinet, and so on. Evolvex also accepts a sketch of what you'd like by mail, email, or telephone. The company boasts that it outperforms the discount giant Ikea. In 2012, Evolvex received the Australian Business Awards for "Best New Product" and "Product Innovation."

Another great example of a custom manufacturer serving both the consumer and business-to-business markets is ATS Acoustics. Located near Chicago, with close to 30 employees, the rapidly growing company delivers customized acoustical products, including sound-absorbing wall panels. Like Evolvex, the customer is able to design the acoustic panels online and, along with color and size, can choose the look and feel of the fabric. The customer can even get an image or photograph printed on the product. The company provides kits to designers and architects, giving them the ability to design the product. And, while the company has a high degree of expertise to share, it remains dedicated to empowering customers to make decisions and choose what they want. Its employees take pride in their ability to adapt and alter their approach to respond to and empower their customers, including Bose, Starbucks, Warner Brothers, and The Voice.

The company's founder, Mark Aardsma, is passionate about listening and paying attention to the customer. He even refuses to employ voice prompt technology. When someone calls the company, a live voice promptly answers the phone. The company is well aligned to the customer motivation of attention, which shows in everything its employees do.

There are many other examples of companies that are great customizers of their product or service. From small companies like ATS Acoustics, Evolvex, WeBobble, and Customized Girl to larger companies like Lands' End, success in delivering the brand intention of customization requires a focus on what the customers and clients want and the empowerment that comes with it. To win requires consistently taking the idea of *it's all about listening to the customer* to a higher level than your competitors.

PREEMINENCE

Preeminence defines the brand intention of products or services that deliver superiority, high levels of expertise, and competency. It offers products that are innovative, unique, cutting edge, and revolutionary. Preeminent services deliver high levels of competency, aptitude, know-how, excellence, and capability. *The customer motivation in the brand intention of preeminence is competency.* Preeminence offers a sense of predictability, control, and accomplishment. As a customer, I feel competent that I made the right choice.

A few years ago, Karl Sigerist, the President and CEO of Crelogix, a Canadian company that provides consumer credit services, told me that although his company's goal was to deliver superior products or services, he preferred not to use the term "superior," as it might make his employees believe they could rely on the level of product or service already achieved. As a result, the company might not continue to innovate and create new and advanced products or services. He sought alternative ways to express the ongoing pursuit of superiority.

I began to explore the different ways to express the idea of superiority and, eventually landed on the term preeminence, which conveys the distinction, uniqueness, prominence, renown, and excellence that business leaders strive for. One outcome of this exercise was the realization that whatever word you choose to describe your brand intention is fine, as long as it accurately articulates and conveys the value you're striving to deliver to the customer and how you align your internal communication to the company and team. The six brand intentions do not change nor does their alignment to the three customer motivations. The following example demonstrates the many ways in which preeminence can be articulated.

BMW does not sell a car; it sells the "ultimate driving machine." For years, it was difficult to find an advertisement or marketing piece referring to a BMW as a car. Over a period of over five years, we discovered only two ads that did. The same is true of Apple. When you walk into an

Apple store, the alignment to its preeminent brand intention is obvious. The clean and simple configuration of the store and the clean lines of its tables convey the company's objective of removing clutter from the customer experience. As discussed in Chapter Three, the company is driven by its desire to amaze and separate itself from the pack. At the store level, this alignment extends its image of innovation and uniqueness. As a customer, if your laptop isn't working properly, you don't go into one of its stores expecting to have it serviced; there is no customer service or repair department. Instead, there is a "genius bar," and "you'll need an appointment to speak to a "genius." This expression of preeminence reminds you of how good they are.

When it comes to service providers, preeminence is expressed by exceptional knowledge and expertise. Unlike alignment to the brand intention of customization, where the customer provides the solution, alignment to preeminence means the customer expects the provider to create the solution. Accounting, legal, and consulting firms often fall into this category.

Companies that develop and deliver tailored software applications for financial and healthcare institutions, and government entities, among others, are typically providers of what are referred to as custom solutions. Even if the software is part of an off-the-shelf program, it may require tailoring, alterations, and changes to accommodate an organization's needs. Often, the software developer creates software specific to a single customer's needs or requirements. This is an often overlooked form of preeminence. In brief, preeminence typically exists when the customer relies on the provider of a product or service to deliver the competency, expertise, and know-how to create a solution, implement a strategy, solve a problem, or obtain a necessary service. Outsourcing is often used to accomplish one or more of these.

An example of a powerful service provider that touts its preeminence is SAP. The 40-year old company is the world's largest provider of enterprise software and software-related services. Other examples are McKinsey and Company, Ernst and Young, and Bain and Company.

Another well-known brand delivering preeminent consumer and professional products is Bose. Founded by MIT professor Dr. Amar Bose, the company is a brand leader in home and professional audio technology and products. While audio devotees may believe there are better products at comparable or more competitive pricing, Bose has done an exceptional job of marketing its brand value.

Bose's prowess reaches beyond the audio products for which it is famous. It has branched out to develop and deliver test instruments for materials research and product development, as well as a shock-and-vibration system that offers protection to cargo carried by the heavy-duty trucking industry. While there is always a degree of risk associated with expanding a brand to other product or service strategies, if your new product or service is aligned to your already existing brand intention, it can be successful. In contrast, if McDonald's began offering a high-priced gourmet burger, it would be a recipe for failure.

Like many providers of preeminent products, Bose is able to price its product and enjoy margins that reflect the customer's perception of the preeminent value of its product. In maximizing its margin, it is able to invest in furthering its strong market presence, support its research and development efforts, and continue to build its brand in the manner required to sustain its brand intention. Customers are willing to pay for the value they expect and receive and that best responds to their motivation and emotional fulfillment.

LOW PRICE

Low price defines the brand intention of products or services where price is the main consideration. The customer motivation in the brand intention of low price is competency. Low price offers a sense of predictability, control, and the accomplishment in getting the best deal. *It satisfies the human need and desire to feel competent, coping, and good at what we do.* As a customer, I feel competent that I got the best deal, was a smart shopper, or paid the least possible amount for the product or service.

There are many companies that fit this bill. Wal-Mart immediately comes to mind because it does it so well. By the numbers, as of February 28, 2013, the company has 10,626 locations around the world. In 2012, company-wide sales topped $460 billion. The expectation of a Wal-Mart customer is to get the lowest price.

Behind Wal-Mart's success is a relentless company-wide ambition to innovate to maximize the cost-to-goods-sold ratio. Among the many things the company does well is keep the costs associated with its supply chain management low. Whether that means automating its warehouse and distribution, dictating price and packaging specifications, or taking over a market, Wal-Mart approaches everything with a can-do attitude that borders on obsession. The result is that the company is very good at creating the outcome intended by a price leader.

The brand intention of low price is about attracting customers by predictably offering the lowest price possible and leaving your competitors with little option other than to try to match your prices. The main goal is to gain customers and take market share. While the other five brand intentions can be used to create and grow a niche and, eventually become a market leader, the low price leader's quest is to build volume.

The definition of trust lies in the promise to give the customer the lowest price. Hence, many low-price competitors go so far as to guarantee the low price and honor coupons or match the discounts their competitors are offering. This "we'll match or beat them every time" attitude convinces the customer to trust the brand.

Commodities most often fall into the low-price category and reflect the supply–and-demand approach to price setting. The relationship of price to availability and scale demonstrates that leveraging the economies of scale in the successful pursuit of low-cost strategies is vital to success. Other equally important strategies include operating efficiencies, mass buying power, control over vendors, and the ability to leverage low-profit margins in relationship to sales volume. The thinking behind this brand intention is that five percent of $5 million ($250,000) is better than seven percent of $3 million ($210,000). Smaller companies competing for market share do not have the same economies of scale and, over time, cannot compete. If a low-price leader like Wal-Mart, Aldi, Costco, Amazon, or Ikea, knowing it can operate more effectively and grow with slimmer margins, chooses to do so, it can lower prices to a level that competitors are unable to sustain. As a result, they take market share, often causing their competition go out of business.

Whether a company provides a consumer-based product or service or business-to-business products or services, there are other routes it can take when competing on price to protect a specific market share and retain higher margins. "Value-add" offerings and marketing can sometimes be used to compete against the lowest price leader and maintain and grow a niche market. For example, Toyota was a low-price competitor that strategically developed its offerings to sell a cousin to low price, low cost of ownership. To compete with Wal-Mart's warehouse brand Sam's Club and differentiate themselves, Costco offers a sampling of better quality and more select products. The appeal of better quality and an increased level of service attracts customers for whom these are worthwhile considerations.

Other examples include a builder who offers timely project completion or superior craftsmanship as a means to win business, even if the bid is only slightly higher or a trucking company that promotes timeliness and promises lower freight damage can separate themselves from lower priced competitors. Many entrepreneurs and small business owners, as well as many established larger companies, struggle to come to terms with changing strategies when a low-price competitor cuts into their market share by taking away customers and attracting new ones. It's an important decision whether to innovate and change to compete on price or to further separate oneself from the low-price competitor to sustain and grow on one of the other five brand intentions. Whatever the decision and regardless of the size of your company and market, clarity and alignment to your brand intention is necessary for success.

Another aspect of low price needs to be considered. What the customer gains from getting the best price is often offset by the perception of poor service and lack of attention. Low- price providers are often seen as "win at any cost" competitors, leaving customers questioning whether the company cares enough about them and their employees. The drive for leanness and operational excellence can result in customer dissatisfaction, leading them to pay a bit more somewhere else to get their needs met. These important considerations should not be overlooked.

Some believe that eventually all products find themselves becoming a commodity. If a particular product does not undergo significant change and advancement, the options for how to compete become limited and eventually low price is the only path to success. This thinking often gets companies that rely on one of the other five brand intentions in trouble. Mobile phones are a good example. Nokia has found itself trying to keep up with Samsung and Apple, each of which is focused on continuous preeminence. They define market leadership in different terms and keep focused on brand intention. If Nokia is unable to keep up, it may find itself gravitating toward becoming competitive on price.

The lesson is that the brand intention of low price, like the other five, is best served when it is pursued by choice, rather than imposed by market forces.

PHYSICAL WELLBEING

Physical wellbeing defines the brand intention of products or services that deliver improved bodily health and contribute to the customer's physical welfare. It offers improved appearance, fitness, strength, and sometimes vigor; it can also be used to offer environmental comfort and safety. *The customer motivation in the brand intention of physical wellbeing is caring* for oneself and others. A part of our self-concept is how healthy we feel and how good we look. At a deeper psychological level, *physical wellbeing satisfies the human need and desire to care of oneself and others we care about.*

As mentioned in Chapter Two, Whole Foods is a good example of a company that successfully delivers on the brand intention of physical wellbeing. Founded by John McKay in 1980, it offers its customers the highest quality natural and organic products available and shows the same level of caring to all its stakeholders. It is devoted to organic farming, seafood sustainability, humane animal welfare practices, promoting health and education, and caring about the environment. It has over 300 stores in the United States and is expanding into the United Kingdom and Canada. In 2012, its revenue topped $11.5 billion. The company's vision is to expand to 1,000 stores worldwide.

Whole Foods expresses a commitment to caring for the health of its customers and the planet. It is summed up in an interdependent philosophy of good food, good people, and a good earth. Whole Foods provides a model for any business that is seeking to align the various facets of how it operates, including how to align its vendors, sources, and assorted other suppliers. Whole Foods communicates its mission and values to its customers and marketplace very well. Much like Harley-Davidson, Apple, Lands' End, or any great brand, it has achieved a remarkable alignment with its customers, who are willing to pay for the emotional connection.

Whole Foods employees are exceptionally well aligned to the brand intention. When a customer asks for assistance in finding a particular item, rather than telling the customer the location of the item (Whole Foods stores do not have aisle numbers), the team member (the term the company uses for its employees) stops what they are doing and walks you to it. In all likelihood, they will also start a brief conversation with you, further demonstrating the caring attitude, which is in alignment with the brand intention and is expected from every team member.

At the core of its brand intention and caring is the message of social responsibility and the openness and honesty that it conveys. This aspect of Whole Foods' brand intention can be easily overlooked, yet it is key to the trust and loyalty it engenders and the subtle and powerful message that underscores its brand—that it is open and honest about what it offers and sells unlike all those grocery store chains that, for decades, have been selling you inferior, overprocessed, and sometimes unhealthy food. The emotional element of the differentiator Whole Foods offers engages the competitiveness that we show toward the brands we prefer. Much like Ford vs. Chevy, Coke vs. Pepsi, McDonald's vs. Burger King, and Samsung vs. Apple, the customer takes an active role in supporting the competitor they align with, becoming a fan and advocate for the brand. By shopping at Whole Foods, the alignment of the customer to the brand intention creates the resources necessary to carry on the competition.

Another psychologically compelling example of the brand intention of physical wellbeing is coffee. A couple of years ago I had a toothache that kept me awake for most of the night. I was tired, edgy, and anxious about going to see my dentist. En route to the dentist's office, I stopped and bought myself a double cappuccino in order to feel more awake and energetic. About twenty minutes later, as I sat and nervously waited to have my tooth repaired, I found a magazine whose cover photo was a large coffee sack lying on its side. From it spilled beautifully roasted coffee beans and the headline, "Coffee, the world's drug."

Flipping to the article, I came across a table comparing different sources of caffeine: colas, teas, cocoa and coffee. For each, the chart indicated the type of caffeine, its strength, how long it affected a person's metabolism, and how long after consumption it took to have a physical affect. My anxiety escalated. The caffeine in coffee had a physical affect after 25 to 35 minutes—at just about the time the dentist would be drilling my tooth. Sure enough, just as the dentist began his work, I felt myself becoming more and more restless. I was more anxious and tense than if I had not consumed the coffee.

Like many people, I believed that coffee had an immediate result, in the range of seconds to 5 or 10 minutes. Some people think they can feel the effects with the first sip; some think they can feel a physical response when they inhale the coffee's aroma. This reaction is an example of the physiological influence that is conveyed and leveraged through the brand intention of physical wellbeing.

There's an aspect of confidence that is inherent in feeling healthier, stronger, attractive, and more energetic. The more a brand and its marketing and messaging leverages the psychological impact, the more powerful the brand. Hence the powerful psychological influence of the promise of energy that coffee offers, even though its initial effect is much like a placebo.

In 1984, Folgers coffee introduced the world to its now widely recognized jingle, "the best part of wakin' up is Folgers in your cup." For three decades the jingle has accompanied television advertisements with images of people waking up to the drip of fresh coffee brewing and immediately being welcomed to the new day. Energetic and refreshed by the aroma alone, the ads convey the sense that Folgers will make your day, your relationships, and your work better. More recently, its television commercials depict family members connecting and caring for one another, another reminder of the caring aspect of its brand intention. The emotional aspect of these ads is powerful.

Folgers' approach to marketing has made it America's #1 coffee brand, comprising over 40 percent of the ground coffee market. It did this by competing for market share against many other coffee companies, including Maxwell House, Eight O'Clock, and the gourmet offerings of Peet's and Starbucks. It offers its coffee through retail grocery stores and supermarkets and has created additional revenue streams selling to restaurants and offering gourmet blends and single-cup options. The brand intention of Folgers is so effective it often overcomes the price trends typical of commodity markets (coffee is second only to oil among the top ten most traded commodities worldwide).

The brand intention of physical wellbeing can be applied to many products: skin care brands such as Nivea, Olay, Bath & Body, Burt's Bees, and L'Occitane; diet supplements, vitamins, and many pharmaceutical products; and programs and services that promote stronger and longer lives, such as Weight Watchers and Curves. The latter franchise provides fitness and weight-loss facilities for women. Founded in 1992, its first franchise opened in 1995. Since then, it has expanded to include franchises in 10,000 locations in over 90 countries. Curves offers a variety of programs ranging from thirty-minute workouts to one that includes exercise, a managed diet, and individual coaching. To further the value of its brand, it partnered with the Cleveland Clinic, one of the world's best-known medical facilities, to certify its coaches. In the business-to-business marketplace, the company has developed Curves Wellness, working with insurance providers and employers to improve employee health, decrease absenteeism, and boost productivity.

Physical wellbeing can also be delivered through the products or services that make up and contribute to the customer's environment, among them furnishings and home decorating products that are a part of our living and work spaces. For example, while the ergonomic furniture design has its appearance appeal, the intention is to provide physical comfort.

Another less obvious example of the customer motivation of caring for self and others is a customer service or sales center employing hundreds of phone service and online chat representatives that provides ergonomically designed chairs, desks, and lighting that replicates natural sunlight. This allows its employees to be more comfortable and, in turn, more productive. In the business-to-business arena, Herman Miller, the award-winning furniture company, has established itself as a brand specifically oriented to the ergonomic market. It boasts of its design capabilities and innovative approaches and environmental advocacy. In 2012, the company's revenue topped $1.7 billion. In all of its approaches to business, the company leverages the customer motivation of caring.

Trust is conveyed through a belief that the provider of physical wellbeing will look out for customers' best interest and care for them, regardless of who they are, and that the provider will always be open and honest with them. It's much like going to see a physician. While a doctor may be the most competent, if he doesn't demonstrate a desire to care for you as an individual, you're likely to doubt his true intentions. This sense of trust is the essence of the brand intention of physical wellbeing and applies to consumer and business-to-business markets.

PERSONAL ACTUALIZATION

Personal actualization defines the brand intention of products or services that deliver and support the customer's psychological self-knowledge and development. It offers self-discovery, psychological growth, consciousness, increased self-esteem, and inner peace. The brand intention can also be used to offer improved communication, better relationships, and greater happiness. *The customer motivation in the brand intention of personal actualization is caring for self and others.* When you feel better about yourself and are more in touch with your feelings and emotions and their origins, you are more alive and able to accomplish more. A part of our self-concept is how likeable and lovable we are.. Therefore, the better you know you, the more you can accept and like yourself. At a deeper psychological level, *personal actualization satisfies the human need and desire to love one's self, to be loved and accepted by others for who we are, and to have the ability to be open to accepting and loving others.*

Of the great brand names delivering self-actualization are the giants of self-help, self-improvement, human motivation, and spiritual leadership. Among them are Anthony Robbins, Joel Osteen, Oprah Winfrey, Eckhart Tolle, Dale Carnegie, Stephen Covey, Deepak Chopra, Wayne Dyer, and the Dalai Lama. Sigmund Freud and Carl Jung were two of the great pioneers and influencers of much of the work of personal actualization and self-invention. The breadth and depth of personal programs available worldwide makes it relatively easy for anyone to engage in any form of personal actualization.

Over the last five decades, the market for personal actualization has grown rapidly because of the ever-increasing interest in self-help and self-improvement. Including books, seminars, video products, and personal coaching, the self-improvement industry in the United States in 2012 was estimated to be approximately $11 to $12 billion. As much of the money indirectly and directly spent on personal actualization flows into not-for-profit and religious organizations or is attributed to other industries, such as education, travel and business consulting, this estimate is probably conservative.

Among the range of outcomes that the customer seeks through personal actualization are:

- Managing life's changes
- Growing rich
- Changing one's life
- Becoming a better leader
- Increasing personal effectiveness
- Modifying behavior
- Dealing better with anxiety
- Improving one's love life
- Getting rich quick
- Finding the right mate
- Achieving better life balance
- Leading a fulfilling spiritual life
- Influencing others better
- Living in abundance
- Actualizing one's power
- Overcoming addiction
- Managing conflict more effectively
- Being happier
- Dealing with adversity
- Becoming a better performer
- Overcoming abusive behavior
- Managing stress better
- Attaining the ideal afterlife
- Overcoming loss
- Being more content
- Changing habits
- Finding one's true self
- Improving communication skills
- Finding inner peace, and
- Being a better father, mother, daughter, son, brother, sister, wife, husband, grandmother, grandfather, and friend

My intention is not to poke fun at any of these or devalue them in any way. Rather, my aim is to demonstrate the tremendous range and value that personal actualization provides. Indeed, we are willing to pay well for it, and it provides some of the best margins of any industry today because, for the most part, when customers buy these products or services, they are primarily paying for a concept, philosophy, set of ideas or ideals, program, or process through which they achieve something they feel they lack. Another important aspect of this brand intention is that the primary responsibility for satisfaction resides with the customer and not the provider. The customer determines whether they received the value they expected—their desired outcomes—from their investment of money spent and time committed.

The brand intention of personal actualization has become a prominent fixture for several reasons. Throughout history, religion, philosophy, mythology, and, more recently, psychology have all been means by which we've explored the human endeavor, all with the aim of understanding and knowing ourselves. The origins of self-help date back to ancient Egypt and the Greek and Roman empires. The Christian bible and the story of the life of Jesus Christ ask us to look inward to explore who we are, what our intentions are, and how we can be better servants to one another and to God. Other religions—Hinduism, Buddhism, Islam, and Judaism—also provide a framework for self-discovery and the need to take responsibility for our actions and deeds. They all provide a means through which to evaluate and learn about one's self and to become the person we ideally want to be.

These approaches to understanding human behavior and emotion have helped us to pursue our knowledge of who we are and why we do the things we do. Increased self-knowledge and realizing who we are socially, psychologically, physically, emotionally, and spiritually convey tremendous power. This power lets us choose what we say and do and also allows us to better explore and interpret our own thoughts and to manage what we think. It allows us to manifest the most powerful aspect of human behavior: choice.

In a business-to-business context, employee and leadership development are aspects of personal actualization. Over the past twenty years, much like the personal and life coaching industries have grown, so have the leadership and executive coaching industries. In the United States, the executive coaching industry has grown to over $2.5 billion in annual revenue. Worldwide, coaching is one of the fastest growing industries. Among business leaders and executives, the capability for self-knowledge is a key attribute of success.

This is pretty powerful stuff. Emotional intelligence, social intelligence, emotional maturity, leadership IQ, and interpersonal intelligence are all excellent examples of the level of study, science, and art to which self-knowledge and actualization have been taken in a relatively short time. The formalized study of psychology is only a little over a century old. The products or services that deliver personal actualization are popular for many reasons. Four of these are key. The first is our natural desire to understand ourselves and get the most out of life. Regardless of a person's stature in society, station in life, or personal experience, we all want to get the most from our lives. We all want more and seek that which we feel we deserve. Many products or services providing personal actualization and individual abundance respond to this desire. The idea of personal and professional coaching is now readily accepted, whereas just two decades ago the few who had professional or life coaches weren't ready to let the world know about it.

A second reason for the popularity of personal actualization is the pace of change and complexity of our world. With the ever-increasing speed of change and the bombardment of information and messaging, we seek new ways to cope with the range of demands and multiple activities we engage in. This ongoing challenge has led to the shared understanding that our mental health is a primary contributor to our overall wellbeing. Advances in healthcare and our ability to live longer lives have put mental health center stage because of its influence on the quality of those additional years.

A third reason is our business society and the way we currently live. Before the industrial age, most people engaged in agriculture. The increasing need to grow crops to feed and clothe the growing population led to many of the mechanical and technical inventions that resulted in the industrial revolution. As our capability for technological development increased, we moved into the information age that has further increased the pace of innovation and change. One of the greatest challenges we face is how to manage and use all the information and knowledge available to us. Going forward, the range of choices is not likely to lessen, thereby requiring us to be much more aware of how we use all the information and content we have access to, as well as how to use our increased capacity to communicate over distance, over time, and with larger numbers of people. We may look back on this time as a transition from the information age to the age of awareness. Our times require that we find ways to deal with these challenges.

A fourth influence is the Baby Boomer generation's interest in self-help and self-improvement. This was as much a result of timing as it was the influence of the changes that rippled through society. Knowledge of psychology was expanding, resulting in an increased understanding of human behavior. In addition, during the late 1950s, 1960s, and 1970s, experimentation with hallucinogens and other substances offered this generation the opportunity to explore and access experiences far beyond what earlier generations experienced. Add to this the Cold War and the increased awareness of the environmental impact of industrial expansion, the AIDS epidemic, the ever-increasing pace of change and innovation, and societal change, and it's no wonder people wanted to better understand their personal relationship to life.

The experience of the Baby Boomer generation, with its increasing interest in products and services offering self-actualization, was passed on to the Millennials. Many of the tendencies toward self-expression and the advocacy of communicating emotion have become a cornerstone of the generation and contribute to the open sharing of imaginative ideas. All of this encourages even higher levels of innovative and creative thinking that further fuel the future of our business society. By adding the expanding capability of today's communication technology, you can see what a powerful offering personal actualization will continue to be.

The six intentions provide the framework for identifying the main ingredient a product or service represents. In service to the main ingredient, aspects of the other five can be applied in varying degrees to increase its value and convey additional customer satisfaction. Often, using one or two intentions in support of the main offering is referred to as a value-add. A word of caution—the main brand intention must be able to stand alone. Trying to be everything to everyone is a dangerous strategy. This is often a hard lesson for leaders and their companies to learn.

The six brand intentions allow us to readily identify the key emotional motivation of the customer that is present and represented in each (Figure 5.1). These become an important aspect in the design of not only the product or service. They are also important in how the product or service is delivered and how all team members and the organization behave in alignment and support of the intention. Whether it is a large multinational corporation or a small business in a local community, every great brand that enjoys customer trust and loyalty demonstrates this alignment.

Human Motivation	Customer Motivation	Brand Intention
Importance	Attention	Community
		Customization
Competency	Competency	Preeminence
		Low Price
Acceptance	Caring	Physical Wellbeing
		Personal Actualization

Figure 5.1   The Alignment of Customer Motivation and Brand Intention

In the following chapter, we'll explore some well-known brands, as well as some smaller companies that you may not know, and look into the unique recipes that make them great. We'll identify the customer motivation and how it translates into brand intention.

SIX

Extraordinary Brand Recipes

We hunger for great recipes.

What makes a brand extraordinary? What differentiates it from its competitors? Why do we respond to powerful brands as we do? What is in the secret sauce of winners? Why do we want to associate with the best? What do extraordinary brands have that the others don't?

Again and again we ask these questions. We want to know how to replicate that high level of success and make it our own. Whatever role we have in a company or team, we all aspire to be a part of something extraordinary.

First, extraordinary companies with extraordinary brands are well aligned. Their cultures and leadership are aligned to the company's brand intention, which delivers in alignment to what the customer is buying.

Second, the company has a unique recipe, and the main ingredient is clearly articulated, understood, and focused on. The priorities of what to focus on in creating and delivering the company's products or services are known to everyone, and all act in alignment to that set of priorities. A sense of individual and shared commitment exists among company or team members, regardless of role or function, to relentlessly pursue and deliver the main ingredient to the customer.

While this may appear complex, it doesn't have to be, and the simpler the message, the more customers are able to see and feel the difference. Simplicity is one of the attributes of extraordinary brands. Complexity in a product or service often makes the customer anxious. While we like to have choices, having too many choices is not a good idea.

Have you ever felt uncomfortable when someone tries to sell you something with a lot of add-ons or options? Do you ever find yourself questioning the motives of the seller? When we're given too much to think about, being sold too much, or being sold something more complicated than we want, we tend not to trust the seller or not trust our own ability to make the right choice.

If the provider of a product or service claims that it will fulfill all your needs, that's a pretty high mark to reach. You are likely to respond skeptically. I am not saying it's not possible; I am saying it is highly unlikely. Therefore, we're less likely to trust it.

Potentially, a customer may lack confidence in a company that offers a little bit of everything or tries to sell an overly broad range of products or services. We tend to place more trust in those that work to master a particular product, service, technology, or expertise. If a company offers a little of everything, it increases the likelihood that it's not going to be great at any of them. The one exception is a low-price provider from which the customer is not expecting a high degree of product knowledge or service competency.

Chapter Four explored brand intention and the power of the main ingredient. Chapter Five examined the six brand intentions and the alignment to the three customer motivations. This chapter explores what it takes to create and articulate an extraordinary brand intention. We'll investigate a set of powerful brand intentions, identify the main ingredient, and learn how aspects of the other intentions are used to complement the main ingredient to further attract the customer (see Figure 6.1). We'll identify what the customer is motivated by and emotionally responds to, and, ultimately, what the customer trusts.

I have selected small-to-large multinational corporations to give you insight into how alignment works across all companies and teams, regardless of size. The elements of the Business Code and characteristics of alignment apply to any company, any team, and any business.

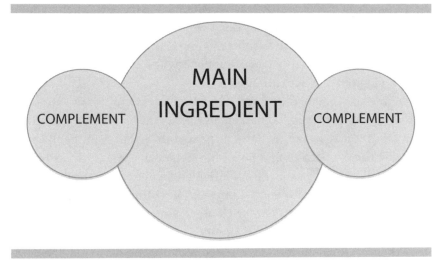

Figure 6.1　The Unique Recipe

A PASSION FOR MUSIC

I once read a poem in which the author compared walking into a bookstore to walking into a bakery, the scent of books evoked the emotion associated with the familiarity and anticipation of a fine bakery. He wrote that opening a book's cover was like breaking into a freshly baked loaf of bread and that flipping through a book and stopping at a page and reading was like taking the first bite. It was satisfying and tasty; it invited you to want more, to take another bite, to turn to the next page.

This is the experience I have every time I enter Wildwood Guitars. Occupying a small storefront, the shop is located in the center of my community. Whenever I set foot into Wildwood, I sense its uniqueness. By today's standards, its approximately 500 square feet is a small space from which to conduct a thriving, rapidly growing retail business. It is also part of its charm and likely contributes to the concentrated, alluring aroma of the fine woods and finishes emanating from the guitars hanging on the walls. As customers walk into the store and across the old worn Italian rugs, they are quickly and warmly greeted by the artists sitting at the four desks that have, over the years, replaced the counters and display cases that once occupied the space. Calling them sales clerks (they don't have official titles) would be a gross understatement. Each is an accomplished player, who leaves customers marveling when demonstrating a particular guitar. They don't sell. They help you choose the guitar that's right for you, that best fits the music you want to create. As they will tell you with conviction, it's not about buying just any guitar. It's about the art and your self-actualization.

When you enter Wildwood Guitars, it doesn't cross your mind that it is a thriving leader in its market, an important player in a worldwide industry. Yet it is one of the largest independent sellers in the world. It achieved this by becoming a powerful niche player in an industry that has moved rapidly toward consolidation and where big is the norm.

The world's largest retailer of musical instruments is Guitar Center. Owned by Bain Capital, "Guitar Center plunged into the new millennium with the forward-moving momentum of the previous decade and a vision of vast expansion." Compared to Wildwood Guitars, the company is a giant, easily the Wal-Mart or Best Buy of music, with over 239 locations in the United States and over $2 billion a year in revenue. The company proves that a low-price brand intention and the ability to offer a large selection of items and brands can be a sustainable and growth oriented path to success. Throughout its history, Guitar Center has grown through a strategy of leveraging acquisitions and opening new stores. Like all great businesses, even large volume players need to change to succeed. Any great company must innovate and evolve to be competitive long term, and Guitar Center has proven it can adapt. It has an operational capability and efficiency enabling it to quickly distribute its merchandise to the store level, to move it from store to store, and to swiftly respond to its customers. As part of its vision, the company states, "Guitar Center has no intention of slowing down and will be around for generations to come."

The difference in Wildwood Guitar's approach to how the customer is treated and the intention of its brand couldn't be any more different than Guitar Center's, whose stated main customer objective is "to provide for the musician's every need." As a result, it offers a broad array of products—keyboards, drums, audio equipment, DJ turntables—pretty much anything you're looking for. Guitar Center is a low-price retailer with an extensive selection, touting discount pricing. Customer service is naturally in alignment to that intention. While the sales associates at Guitar Center receive product knowledge training, they most often help customers find a particular product from the extraordinary range of choices and fill the role of sales clerk.

The big-box effect and low-price brand intention isn't lost on the customer. It is further reinforced by a narrow exit, in some instances complete with turnstiles, that is designed for theft-prevention and is manned by a sales associate checking the customer's receipt against the items carried out the store. The low-price brand intention influences the sales associates and their perspective on the company's culture.

The contrast with Wildwood Guitars couldn't be any starker. While many of the influences of big-box retailing have found their way into the marketing of retail musical instruments (including competition on price and volume), Wildwood has resisted this impulse and has successfully held its own. In fact, it has done much better than that. It has become one of the most trusted independent guitar dealers in the world by carving out a niche that has resulted in a consistent growth. Year to year over the past decade, it has experienced double-digit growth by focusing on selling guitars, a narrow selection of high-quality amplifiers, and a few select accessories. It has moved away from selling low-priced items and taken a boutique approach by offering high-quality, vintage, custom, and rare guitars.

Wildwood is currently the largest Fender Custom Shop seller in the world. Among independent dealers, it consistently ranks among the top providers of Fender, Gibson, Taylor, and several other well-known brands. Among guitar makers, it has achieved an elevated status, resulting in several lines of "custom" guitars that include the Wildwood brand in their model names. The average price of a guitar sold at Wildwood is between $3,000 and $4,000.

Steve and Marilynn Mesple founded Wildwood Guitars in 1985. Steve has had "a lifelong love affair with music and guitars." Their approach was to "sell the greatness and goodness of guitars." Steve sees anyone at any level of playing ability as a fellow artist and friend. Exploration and choice are key motivators to the self-actualizing artist. The same is true when an artist buys a guitar.

Steve's leadership approach and its influence on his team at Wildwood are evident and is an excellent example of a leader's influence on the customer relationship, brand, and culture. A team member told me, "I don't offer my customer a guitar because of the make. The guitar is the vehicle through which the art is created. Helping the customer find the right guitar for their art and for what they're trying to do is what matters." This attitude creates a connection and brings meaning to every customer interaction.

The relationship between Wildwood Guitars and its customers centers on the trust that comes from caring. Customers from far and wide interact with the artists who make up Wildwood's team and, by phone and email, making buying decisions based on their input and recommendations. The members of the team build relationships, carefully listening to what the customer is looking for from a particular instrument—what they play, what they want to achieve, and what they aspire to—as well as what the customer likes in a guitar, including how it looks, feels, and sounds. Without ever playing the instrument, the customer makes a decision. That level of trust is compelling and is evidence of the caring nature of the Wildwood brand. It explains why the vast majority of Wildwood's sales are not in-store. Steve makes it very clear. "We never try to sell the customer anything that they don't want to buy . . . period. That's not who we are and it's not what our customers would ever expect from us. Everyone here knows that's not something we would ever do."

Steve Mesple has made changes along the way. And while they didn't always get the results he was looking for, he has worked toward always making changes consistent with what motivates his customers, the alignment to the business's brand, and what he sees as an unwavering culture of passion. He's carefully recruits the right people for his team and rewards them for their passion and dedication. With the advent of the Internet, he expanded his sales capabilities and reach. The store's website now offers over 2500 videos of great guest artists playing Wildwood's offerings. The videos are not just entertaining. They are educational, inspirational, and in service to the customer. As Steve told me, "People love to hear great guitars played by great artists. It gives them the opportunity to experience what we can offer them, which is an unparalleled inventory of amazing guitars and trust. And we do it with unbridled passion."

To compete with the appeal of the Wildwood Guitars of the world, Guitar Center offers through its brand Musician's Friend, a single-person sales unit called Private Reserve. It is located in a small section of its large distribution center in Kansas City, Missouri. Customers can call and speak directly to the person at Private Reserve and get the expert assistance of an artist in the selection and buying of a custom or high-priced guitar. In relation to its brand and the perception of its customers, Private Reserve is much like a small stand-alone brand that lives within the larger brand intention of Guitar Center. While it offers a distinct service and product, the customer may not intuitively or intellectually find it to be in alignment with their interpretation of the Guitar Center and Musician's Friend overall brand intention.

At the core of Wildwood's achievement and the success of Guitar Center is what lies at the heart of the success of any business. It is alignment. For any enterprise, large or small, competing in a local, regional, or global marketplace, the required ingredient is the alignment of the customer's expectation and their experience of how it is delivered. This means that the company's people work with one another and act toward the customer in alignment with the brand intention and the customer's expectations.

THE WORLD'S FAVORITE COFFEE SELLER

In Chapter Five, I introduced the brand intention of physical wellbeing and the physical and psychological effects of the world's favorite drug. I also introduced to Folgers Coffee. By 1984, when the iconic jingle was introduced, the over 100-year old company was owned by Procter & Gamble. Through its catchy jingle, the Folgers brand, which by that time was a constant presence on grocery store shelves, was about to become further embedded in the American consumer's psyche.

A year earlier Howard Schultz, the owner of a small coffee shop in Seattle, had spent time in Italy, where he was intrigued by its engaging coffee shop culture, especially its communitarian nature, and decided to bring that culture to his shop back home. He loved coffee and had worked for a small coffee roaster in Seattle called Starbucks. To further leverage his idea, he bought Starbucks.

Folgers and Starbucks are great examples of how two companies, selling the same basic product can go in significantly different directions. Beyond their shared product and customer affect, the two companies are strategically dissimilar and, over the last three decades, have traveled different paths.

Since 1984 Folgers has grown into a company that enjoys annual revenue of $2 billion dollars and, according to the company, is America's #1 coffee brand. Like any great company, large or small, it has accomplished this by consistently investing in the marketing of its brand identity. It continues to pursue its vision as an iconic brand and has successfully competed for market share against a host of other coffees sold through retail grocery stores and supermarkets. It has also developed a number of additional revenue sources. Recently, the company successfully entered the K-cup, single-serving category. The company's advertising continues to leverage the familiarity of its jingle, the physical wellbeing intention it conveys, and competitive pricing.

Folgers strategic direction has not changed much through the years. After P&G bought the company in 1963, it grew in market share. Since its merger into the J.M. Smucker Company, it continues to compete as it did some thirty years ago against other mainstays of the retail coffee market as well as against the other coffee brands that are part of the Smucker's family of products, including Dunkin Donuts, Kava, Millstone, Medaglia D'Oro, and Café Bustelo.

Meanwhile, Starbucks has become a global powerhouse. In 2012, its annual revenue topped $13.3 billion. With locations in over sixty countries, it is enjoying steady growth worldwide. The company has over 3,300 locations in the China and Asia Pacific region, and its vision is to top 20,000 locations worldwide by 2014. Starbucks is also on retail store shelves and has entered the single-cup category selling its own branded coffee machine. Consistent with its brand intention, the company's single-serve machine is priced slightly higher than its competitors'. The company forecasts that its entry into this market will eventually deliver a multibillion dollar revenue source.

Instead of taking the traditional route and attempting to create inroads into supermarkets and grocery stores, the company took the unique strategic path of offering indulgence on every street corner. Adopting the European community model, Schultz and his company reinvented the coffee market. The emotional connection that Starbucks offers responds to the customer motivation for community and is quite powerful. While some customers say that they feel more alive and charged just smelling the aroma as they walk into the store, it is the connection to the brand

and the experience of the customer that creates the connection the company focuses on. The hot coffee in a recyclable cup is served by baristas (as servers are called), who smile, connect, and convey how much they care about the customer. Through this experience, the customer is further connected to the brand and its promise and, as a result, is willing to pay more for it.

As Starbucks gained in popularity, some critics and customers referred to the brand as the "$5 cup of coffee." This, despite the fact that most of its products were priced well below $5. The label is the result of the emotional bond that occurred between barista and customer and the powerful caring relationship it created. The latte likely costs less, and because the customer is so well cared for, he reciprocates by leaving the change. Hence, the popular perception of the $5 cup of coffee. One might say that Starbucks reinvented retail sales tipping along with the coffee market because the practice has spread to sandwich shops, donut shops, fast food stores, and even dry cleaners and laundries. Even when using a credit or debit card, most provide an opportune place to add a gratuity to your receipt. The customer motivation of connection and community sharing is also the fuel behind the success of the Starbucks gift card. The company estimated that one out of every ten Americans received a Starbucks gift card during the 2012 holiday season.

Starbucks' unique recipe begins with the main ingredient of coffee and then leverages the brand intention of community. It offers a quality product and then adds the complement of customization. Customers are given a set of options—drink type, size, added flavorings, type of milk, and toppings—and can customize their drink. They can enjoy their drink, sometimes with friends, and experience the sense of community. While it's not the same community feeling Harley-Davidson riders enjoy at larger gatherings, a Starbucks store offers a place to meet with friends and business colleagues and get away from it all for a while. The company sees itself as being in service to the communities and neighborhoods it serves inasmuch as it provides a product.

The unique recipe for Folgers Coffee brand intention begins with the same product offering, yet it is much different than Starbucks'. While Starbuck's offers the brand intention of community, Folgers focuses on the delivery of physical wellbeing at competitive pricing and reflects its need to grow through volume. As we'll discover in Chapter Seven, this is not always an easy strategy. However, through strong marketing and powerful brand recognition, Folgers has done it exceptionally well.

THE CONSULTATIVE SELLING OF PREEMINENCE

Mike Fleming is the founder of Decision Point Associates, Inc. Located in Denver, Colorado, Decision Point is a small boutique firm providing hazard recognition education, training, and coaching to improve workplace safety. The company's mission is to prevent workplace incidents that harm people, the environment, and the assets and reputations of its clients, which include ExxonMobil, Weyerhaeuser, Shell, Ashland, BP, Ensign International, and FMC.

Over time, Decision Point has developed a unique and powerful recipe for its brand intention. It brings together preeminence, customization, and aspects of physical enrichment that transcend a variety of industries, countries, and cultures. As a result, in a market crowded with low-price products and training systems, Mike and his team have successfully carved out a niche as one of the world's leading providers of highly effective safety and safety leadership education and development programs.

Mike told me that the bottom line of his product or service is to develop the competency in the client's workforce, which was not always as simple as it sounds: It's hard to sell someone a better way to do something when they think they already know how it's best done. Decision Point's clients often expect that the company's product or service will be customized to their way of doing things. This is often a point of contention and conflict between professional service providers and their customers. Not managing it well often leaves the customer confused and dissatisfied.

Mike lets his clients know that he's not interested in replacing their processes or systems. Rather, by understanding how they do things, he can offer them ways to make improvements aligned with their goals. In most instances, he's able to demonstrate how his clients can incorporate Decision Point's more advanced tools and approaches to get better results. This form of consultative selling is not prescriptive. Mike begins with questions as a way to establish collaborative approaches and ascertain how he can best offer the expertise and know-how of his company and trainers. And, because the approaches different groups within the same client company use may differ from one another, collaboration is often the only way to achieve success.

The main ingredient is the preeminence of Decision Point's advanced and universally applicable tools and expertise. In service to it, the vital aspect of customization is conveyed by tailoring how the methods and tools are applied and how the education is delivered. The ability to collaborate and be flexible in tailoring the program to the customer sometimes leads clients to initiate changes in their processes. When the client is resistant, inviting collaboration is often the only way that Decision Point gets the customer to see things from a different perspective and to invest in effective and sustainable change.

If you add the element of physical wellbeing conveyed through the desire to prevent harm to people and environmental damage and to protect the client's assets and reputation, you have a great recipe. While the main ingredient is the preeminence of the tools, methods, and processes Decision Point offers and delivers, it doesn't hurt to add other ingredients in service to it. As Mike pointed out, "We often find ourselves moving between our way and their way. We know our way is better and sets the standard. That's why they came to us. Through collaboration and some tailoring, we can get them to self-identify ways to improve how they do things. The bottom line is developing sustainable competency in the client's workforce."

A great deal of Mike's and Decision Points' success can be attributed to the ability to successfully engage in consultative selling. It's easy for professional service firms, large and small, to suffer from misalignment because they a lack a clear articulation of what a tailored or customized solution is. For Decision Point, as for any firm offering preeminence, the definition reflects the application of expertise, knowledge, and skills for the purpose of solving the customer's problem and providing a better and improved way to do things. This definition can include a range of services or products. The key consideration is that the customer is relying on the expertise of the provider. This is often confused with the consultative selling approach that relies on the customer's expertise, knowledge, and skills, and results in an offering that is customized to the wants of the customer.

We are in the midst of an explosion of small and single-person companies providing the spectrum of professional services and IT solutions. Often, disagreement and unnecessary conflict, both internally and with customers, results because of a lack of clarity about what the customer is seeking and buying. Consultative selling can be used for either of the two brand intentions, preeminence or customization, yet it is very important that everyone is clear about what is being sold and bought.

For larger companies that are professional service and solution providers, it may at times be even more difficult to achieve the necessary clarity and alignment to preeminence. Among the companies that do it well are McKinsey and Company, IBM, Oracle, SAS, and Boston Consulting Group. A company that clearly articulates it well is SAP. The German multinational company makes enterprise software that helps its customers manage business operations and customer relations. It has several offerings ranging from resource planning software to integration services that allow for the use of its product with other software that a customer may already have running. The company offers what it believes to be the standard for business operations, often asking the customer to tailor operations to conform to its software. This is in alignment with its endeavor to change the way business is done.

SAP takes the approach of applying its expertise and know-how to the process of collaborating with its customers and creating solutions together. In support of this, the company has research and development labs throughout the world. As a complement to its preeminent approach to solutions, it has developed the SAP Community Network, a community of customers, employees, and partners, who engage in a variety of forums—information exchange, education, discussions, as well as the exchange and sharing of technologies—that allow them to communicate and share with one another. All this is aligned to support and expand a multinational company that in 2012 enjoyed $21 billion in revenue.

Both SAP and Decision Point Associates are well aligned to the main ingredient of preeminence. Both are in the business of providing products or services that offer innovative solutions to their customers and both are well-respected market leaders. Both focus on collaborating with their customers to find the solution that best fits and integrates with the customer's way of doing things. Both leverage a multinational community of experts. And both are not afraid to use their expertise and knowledge to lead their customers to explore and embrace better ways to achieve performance.

IT'S NOT ONLY ROCK 'N' ROLL, IS IT?

During the first decade of the new century, which of the following was the top tour attraction in North America?

- Celine Dion
- Bruce Springsteen
- U2
- The Rolling Stones
- Dave Matthews Band

- The Eagles
- Paul McCartney
- Kenny Chesney
- Madonna

In the music industry, community has long been a cornerstone for branding purposes. After all, that is what the legacy of Woodstock is all about. It's also something that the iconic band The Grateful Dead so naturally leveraged and so well communicated through its community-oriented business model. Long after the band ceased to exist, its community continues to thrive. The community of "Deadheads" not only still buys its music, it supports the various collaborations and solo careers of its members. The Deadheads led the way for many artists and bands to market themselves by building community and the free exchange of music and material. Rather than fighting to protect the sharing of its music, the band and its management encouraged it.

The Grateful Dead's model is replicated by other music artists, including Phish, yet none has succeeded at it better than the Dave Matthews Band, which is why the *Dave Matthews Band finished at the top list*. Between 2000 and 2009, its loyal fans purchased over 11 million tickets. The Dave Matthews Band offers a model of success for other businesses interested in the brand intention of community. In fact, companies eager to engage their current and potential customers are duplicating many aspects of its approach, including open sourcing, crowd sourcing, or immediate access and media sharing.

Early on, the band played for free at universities, colleges, and local events, building a community of followers and fans. It managed its brand much as the Grateful Dead did. The band has freely allowed fans to record its music. Until the mid 1990s, the members allowed people to record directly by sourcing from its sound system. Much like the Deads, its hardcore fans are willing to travel significant distances to see the band play. As the size of the venues grew, the Dave Matthews Band offered reasonable ticket prices to make attending multiple shows affordable and to encourage its community to grow.

In 1998, in response to and in service to the fans and market of the band, a merchandising and ticketing hub and fan club called the Warehouse Fan Association was formed. The company, which is housed in a large business and distribution center in Charlottesville, Virginia, is the creation of the band's manager Coran Capshaw. The first manager of the Dave Matthews Band, Capshaw had history with the Grateful Dead and saw the tremendous opportunity to build the band's brand through community and the then newly burgeoning Internet marketplace. The Warehouse immediately leveraged the capabilities of Internet-based commerce and created an interface with its customers through which communication could occur directly. Capshaw's astute business model was designed to eliminate much of the traditional ticketing and merchandising minutia of the music industry. The Warehouse allowed the band to control the selling of its own merchandise, music, and, most important, the band's merchandise and ticketing prices, which increased its ability to control and maximize profitability.

The Warehouse model delivered other benefits. The community of Dave Matthews Band fans, hungry for more music and merchandise, could now buy directly from the fan association. Live recordings soon became available through the site, creating additional revenue sources beyond the traditional sale of albums and replacing music that had previously been available through community members at no cost. As of 2013, the Warehouse offers 25 volumes of Live Trax, a compilation of live concert recordings. The company takes preorders, allowing for efficient production and inventory management. Fans can also register for presale ticket offers, most of which are in high demand and subject to lottery distribution. All of this creates greater levels of business efficiency, increased leveraging of the community brand intention, and profitability.

The model Capshaw built soon attracted other great artists and the company began marketing its fan clubs and merchandise, which resulted in a new entity, Musictoday, which eventually grew to manage over 500 fan clubs for a wide variety of artists. In 2006, Musictoday was purchased by the concert promoter LiveNation. By then, it was grossing over $100 million per year and growing. In early 2010, LiveNation merged with Ticketmaster entertainment, which now controls event ticketing on a global scale.

Music is art. Business is art. Without the art of business, music would not sustain and grow as an industry. Going forward, the key to the success for the Dave Matthews Band is its ability to create great art and purposefully sustain and grow its community brand intention, although it is now managed through an increasingly complex model. It requires the band's ability, in direct interface with its customers, to convey the emotional aspect that motivates them. In other words, the customer should always come first.

The consistent message these examples of success provide is that whether a company is a group of eight people or 60,000, the basic principles of brand intention alignment, and the alignment to the customer, is a key to success.

The following list of companies—some discussed in this book, some not—includes the brand intention for each. For greater insight, visit their websites to see what has been written about them by other authors, journalists, and bloggers. You will also see their available marketing information and annual reports to determine if your conclusions are the same as mine. Do the same for any other brands you are familiar with and have an interest in, including possible competitors.

• Herman Miller	Physical Wellbeing
• McDonald's	Low Price
• Curves	Physical Wellbeing
• Land's End	Customization
• Samsung	Preeminence
• Oprah	Personal Actualization
• KIA	Low Price
• YouTube	Community
• IKEA	Low Price
• BMW	Preeminence
• Nike	Preeminence
• FarmVille	Community
• Evolvex	Customization
• Aldi	Low Price

- Eckhart Tolle   Personal Actualization
- Amazon   Low Price
- Crelogix   Preeminence
- Evian   Physical Wellbeing
- Bain & Company   Preeminence
- ATS Acoustics   Customization
- Apple   Preeminence
- Gerber Knives   Preeminence
- J.W. Hats   Customization
- Mercedes Benz   Preeminence
- State Farm   Community
- VW   Preeminence
- Disney   Community
- Nivea   Physical Wellbeing
- Wal-Mart   Low Price
- Bose   Preeminence
- Sephora   Physical Wellbeing

All the listed companies and brands have three things in common. First, the brand intention for each is readily recognizable. This means that customers connect emotionally to the motivation each offers and the personal fulfillment that comes with it. Second, each is successful, in great part, because of their alignment of the brand intention and why the customer buys to actual delivery of the product or service. Three, they are successful leaders in their markets.

History tells us that it is difficult to predict where each will end up and whether they will remain leading brands. Current success does not guarantee winning in the future. Continued success requires diligence, perseverance, and a commitment to relentless focus on delivering brand intention to the customer. It requires creativity and innovative thinking and constant curiosity and imagination. One thing is certain; success requires the ongoing conversation of alignment.

Chapter Seven is dedicated to the components of alignment and how extraordinary organizations and teams strive for, attain, and sustain alignment. In defining these components, we'll explore how each becomes a part of the ongoing conversation.

Aligning the Company and Team

Every person, every decision, every action.

The odds of G. Hensler becoming an easily recognizable or household brand are highly unlikely. On the other hand, the chances that you own and wear something the company had a hand in manufacturing is, in fact, quite good. If you bought a leather or canvas belt from one of the specialty retailers found in any mall or from a number of other well-known apparel brands, the odds are pretty good it's a Hensler product. G. Hensler is a great small company. It is excellent at what it does and leverages its brand intention to deliver customized accessories that lead to the overall success of its branded apparel with retail customers.

G. Hensler is also a story of how easily a fast-growing business, regardless of its size, can become misaligned and go off course. It's an example of what can happen, and how successful a business can be, when its leadership identifies its misalignments and realigns.

For small businesses, as well as large corporations, revenue chasing can be a dangerous strategy. When a dog chases a car, it can easily become disoriented and get lost, having expended a great deal of energy on an endeavor with little or no return. The same applies to business. Not only can a company easily go off course, the chase for revenue can often lead to the closing of its doors. Fortunately for G. Hensler, its employees, and its customers, the company's story has a happy ending.

Recognizing accessories as an integral part of the vertical specialty store formula, George Hensler, the founder of Esprit Accessories, set up shop in San Francisco in 1989 and offered the design and delivery of customized fashion accessories. The product blend consisted of handbags and belts. When George began the business, he invited Lisa Rissetto to join him. A graduate of the Fashion Institute in New York, Lisa brought her expertise in merchandising, a sharp eye for recognizing future trends, strong customer relationships, and a keen ability to see how design and business blend. Together, George and Lisa launched the business and, through hard work and determination, put the startup on a path of rapid growth. Through the first 14 years, they achieved a consistently brisk rate of up to 50percent per year growth in revenue, and the company consistently generated healthy profits.

In 2004, Lisa bought the business from George. For all practical purposes, the leadership role had already transitioned to her. Based on her effectiveness and the profitable course of the business, they structured a deal in which Lisa became the company's primary owner and CEO.

The company's model for success was already steeped in its ability to sell its design and merchandising expertise to its customers and consistently deliver a quality product. It established partnerships with customers who looked to Hensler and its designers for guidance on accessories. As Lisa explained, "Our definition differs from providing pure contract manufacturing. Our customers come to us for our specific market knowledge and design capabilities, and our expertise in manufacturing. We know what the trends are and are able to interpret them according to each individual brand we work with."

In 2006 and 2007, the company moved forward on a strategy to increase revenue by taking advantage of selling to big box stores. Throughout its early years, its customers consisted of established specialty retail brands, such as Gap Inc., American Eagle Outfitters, Aeropostale, Express, and other popular names. As Lisa looks back on it, "We saw the opportunity to dramatically increase our revenue by working with the big box discount segment of the market and made a conscious decision to go after it. We didn't see the misalignment."

Selling to the big box retailers differed from selling to and servicing its early customers. Until then, most of its products were delivered directly to customers, often directly to their distribution centers. Selling to larger retailers required establishing and managing inventories and taking on new operational capabilities that were unfamiliar to them, all at much lower margins—a significant shift in how the business was run. It was clear that margins would be much slimmer, yet not fully incorporated into the strategy was the inventory aspect.

The definition of partnership with the big box retailers also differed from the company's relationships with the smaller retailers. At the end of 2006, the company was saddled with inventory from suddenly canceled orders. This was compounded in 2007, when orders for more than 20 percent of the inventory the company produced against confirmed purchase orders were canceled. This unsold inventory presented a liability that could potentially cripple the company. As Lisa explains it,

> Selling off the excess inventory meant getting back about 10% on every dollar that we invested in that inventory. We took a significant loss in 2007. The only way we survived was through a strong cash position. Without it, the business very likely would not have made it. At that point we knew we had to realign the business. Had we not gotten back to aligning to our brand, the business would continue to be in jeopardy. We intentionally let go of a great deal of revenue. We gave up about half of our revenue and went back to creating 100% of our sales from customized contract manufacturing and leveraging our design element in support of it.

Along with slashing revenue, Lisa made several other difficult decisions, including eliminating some positions in the company. She refocused the company's efforts on working with retailers on specific categories and offering design that leveraged their insight into the seasonally changing market. "We offer design insight across categories that our competitors can't and leverage our strong merchandising expertise. We engage retailers in a conversation about how to best maximize the accessories we supply to them. It's a unique category that we know very well and our customer doesn't have to take on the cost internally of leveraging the category. We went back to selling our design and merchandising expertise as opposed to supplying a commodity.

"We also had to realign our culture, which meant realigning our staff. Some of the employees couldn't make the transition and left the company. This was especially true in sales. When we aligned ourselves, we focused with complete clarity on what was in the best interest of the business."

As the CEO of Hensler, Lisa made some difficult choices and led the change necessary to realign her company to its customer and brand intention. The unique recipe of Hensler focuses on a main ingredient of customization, with strong elements of preeminence in design and merchandising expertise. The company also gives its clients a high level of attention. By confronting the company's misalignments, Lisa put the company back on track and secured its future. Five years later, the company's revenue reached its 2007 levels and is once again profitable, growing, and aligned. As a result of the turnaround and success of Hensler, Lisa was able to launch 49 Square Miles, a proprietary wholesale division with its own unique brand that sells high-quality handbags and accessories geared to the high-end specialty store.

As in the case of G. Hensler, misalignment usually results from a combination of factors. It is easy for any team or company to become strategically misaligned. The lure of revenue to support growth and expansion is a powerful force. The idea becomes bigger is better. Sometimes very successful companies develop such confidence that its leaders believe they can diversify company product or service strategy to pursue additional markets. Short-term results, while energizing and encouraging, can often mask the realities of longer-term outcomes and consequences. Sometimes, it's simply the leader's desire to be more aggressive or competitive, or simply to try something new. Frequently misalignment is the result of a single team member or small group that influences a team or company to go in a new direction.

These are a few of the sources of misalignment. Note that they are all the result of human motivation and interaction. It's all about who we are, what we want to achieve, and the natural desire to participate and contribute. By now, you've likely concluded that alignment is not an easy undertaking. If you've gotten to this point, you're right.

The term "alignment" isn't typically used in the business curriculum of colleges and universities, and it doesn't typically show up in executive and leadership development programs. As a result, it is rarely an articulated outcome or goal used for visioning and strategic planning. Nevertheless, it is one of the most important outcomes.

For most leaders and team members, alignment is not part of their ongoing conversation; this is likely one of the key contributors to their misalignment. A lack of alignment, and all the challenges and issues it presents, usually becomes part of the dialogue when leaders and members of their companies and teams are forced into it. It's typically not talked about until it can't be ignored. Then, it's a rude awakening. It often seems sudden, yet we know things don't ever happen overnight. Still, if you ask members of the team or employees in different parts of the company, they are likely to say that they've been dealing with the lack of alignment for some time. They've been observing or taking part in the conflict, struggles, and skirmishes caused by it and wondering what it will all lead to. Like a tsunami caused by an undersea earthquake, the plates of the earth's surface have been slowly shifting for quite some time. Preceding the tidal wave were tremors that, if someone had been paying attention to them, provided signs of what was to come. We often look past or ignore the signals of misalignment until its waves are upon us.

There are other reasons that companies and teams don't pay enough attention to alignment. Here is a short list:

- Everyone is too busy to stop and talk about it.
- Although it's been communicated, we can't expect that everyone is going to hear it or be in on the communication.
- Everyone is hard at work on individual goals and objectives and can't always take the time to communicate to make sure everyone is on the same page.
- We have a lot of other priorities.
- People don't always agree with what is being done or how it is getting done, so misalignments are to be expected.
- Not everyone agrees on the outcomes.
- No one, not even the leaders, is willing to truthfully talk about the conflicts.
- It's someone else's responsibility.
- Not everyone is clear on the vision and strategy.

Unfortunately, one aspect misalignment can never be overlooked. When it is happening, customers sense it. They can feel the misalignment. When a company is aligned, customers emotionally experience the satisfaction of being treated in a way that reflects their expectations of getting what they're paying for. Whether doing business with consumers or in a business-to-business situation, customers know when people act in a manner consistent with, and contributing to, the brand intention and customer satisfaction.

The goal and outcome of alignment is for everyone to act in a manner consistent with the intention delivered through its products or services. Leaders must clearly articulate the intention and communicate it throughout the organization to every person in every corner and in every role. It doesn't stop there.

Alignment is more challenging than just a matter of communication. In a larger context in a bigger company setting, it requires all the leaders of the organization to lead and manage alignment effectively. This includes ensuring that all goals and outcomes at the organizational, unit, group, team, and individual levels are clearly articulated and contribute in an aligned fashion (See Figure 7.1).

When alignment is present, the day-to-day tasks and actions that people undertake are united and aligned with customer expectations and the longer term objectives and outcomes of the business. They are aligned to the brand intention, mission, or purpose of the business and its shared vision.

It is an imperative for any company or team to keep a strategic focus on alignment. And while you may not have started with it in mind, you can always come back to it. Much like Lisa Rissetto and her team at G. Hensler, refocusing on alignment will ultimately reap the benefits of business success and keep your company or team on the right track.

ABOUT THE SCALABLE LEVELS OF ALIGNMENT

Figure 7.1 is a visual interpretation of what I refer to as the scalable levels of alignment. My intention is to provide a snapshot of how alignment occurs in a team or organization and a baseline that is scalable and malleable. In relation to the structure of a team and size of an organization, the framework can be expanded or contracted and shaped in a fashion that best fits the team or organization. Figure 7.1 presents the framework in its simplest form; you can do with it what you like and what best serves you.

I also suggest that you apply terminology that best suits you and your team and that best aligns with your company's culture. For example, if you prefer using mission or purpose to describe your brand intention, do

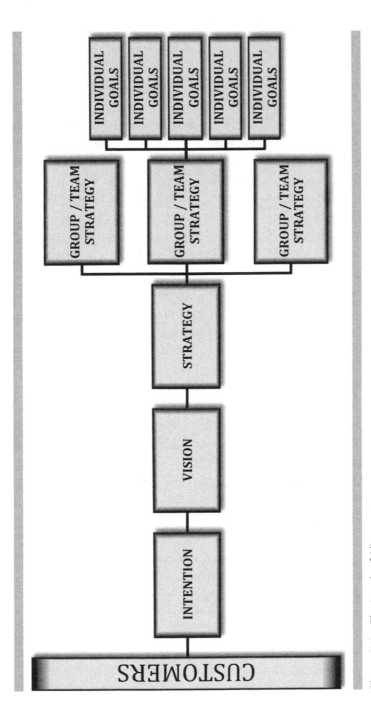

Figure 7.1 The Levels of Alignment

so. Later in this chapter, I'll provide further definitions and structure for how to think about each of the layers, yet I encourage you to use your own words.

The framework is not always a traditional top-to-bottom hierarchal model. Cultures differ. Therefore, I suggest you create the shape and flow that best aligns to yours. Further, based on the preferences of your culture and team, the flow of alignment may not be as linear as it appears in Figure 7.1. For some cultures, the process and flow of alignment may take a spiral, circular, or cyclical form instead. It may be best represented by a set of circles that represent teams or through the use of a nucleus with individual team members or groups in an orbital field. Describe what alignment looks like in your culture and use the framework and integrate processes for planning and communication that best align to it.

Alignment in companies is dynamic in nature. While it begins with the leaders of a company and cascades or moves through its members, any person within the company can affect it. Thinking of alignment in this way creates openness to the ongoing conversation and the informal and fluid communication required for success. It creates an open flow of information, feedback, and ideas. It invites every person to continuously look for and find opportunities to further the company's alignment.

When the ongoing conversation of alignment is alive in a company or team, everyone knows what it looks like, is clear about his or her contribution, and is able to act in the manner that best serves the company and its customer.

ALWAYS STARTING WITH THE END IN MIND

Many leaders with whom I have shared The Business Code put it into action by using it as the framework for visioning and strategic planning. It works well as a planning tool because, at a high level, it asks you to begin with the end in mind. It requires you to consider three key questions: (1) "What are we intending to do?" (2) "Why?" (3) "How do we align everyone to our intention?"

This takes us back to asking and answering the question of why we are in business. The ultimate goal of all businesses, the end game, is to provide a product or service to the marketplace that provides benefit to the customer and that will enable the company to win in the marketplace.

In competition with others, the goal of any business, whether it's a small one-person company or a large multinational corporation, is to win the customer. If you win the customer, they spend money with you instead of your competitors. If you do this well, you get to reap the benefits—profit. You then get to take the profits and, if you choose, reinvest in your business and win more customers and make more money. To do this, you have to get clear on the *what* and *why* of your business. This is all fairly basic and straightforward. What is often overlooked is that success always requires the identification of, agreement on, and successful communication of a brand intention.

A company's brand intention creates a consistent thread of thinking, motivation, and action that makes it possible for every person in the organization at any given time confronted with any circumstance or in any situation to make decisions and act in alignment. From the top down, in any role in the organization, when individuals and groups decide among the options before them, they should be able to identify and take the action that is in alignment. Not just for the purpose of getting something done; rather, they take action and do it in a way that is consistent with the intention and the deliverable to the customer.

Brand intention can take a variety of forms, each of which provides the messaging and articulation of what the company or team aspires to deliver to the market. Whether it is a mission statement, a purpose, a vision, or a code of principles, companies are better aligned when they go beyond their mission or vision statement to clearly articulate their brand intention. The goal of an extraordinary vision or mission statement is to effectively communicate in the most simple and authentic manner the *what* and the *why* of the company and emotionally engage its customers and employees. This is often not as easy as it appears. Saying that your company will be world class, the best in its industry, or the most innovative will likely not communicate what your company has to offer or articulate clearly a desired future state. A firm using a mission statement, "To Be the World's Best Accounting Firm," is not likely to convey its brand intention to its customers. Nor is the intention going to be clear to the firm's members, who are expected to aspire to and fulfill it.

Two aspects of a mission or vision statement are valuable to consider. The first is exploring whether it conveys the emotion and customer motivation of the brand intention. A vision or mission is an important element in how a company communicates its brand. The more it conveys the customer motivation that a company's product or service represents, the greater its ability to emotionally engage the customer. If a mission statement or vision does not accomplish this, it is not the end of the world and it is not an indicator of whether a company is going to be successful or not. On the other hand, when a company's mission or purpose statement is aligned to and clearly articulates its brand intention, the company is that much further along in communicating with its customers and members.

This leads us to the second aspect, which is the influence a mission or vision has on a company's culture. When clearly articulated, the vision or mission provides a focal point and psychological reinforcement for what and why the company exists and acts as steady beacon for alignment. When done well, it contributes to employee engagement and helps to recruit people who are interested in working in a company that is aligned to who they are.

The better a mission statement, vision, or other form of communication connects to customer motivation and brand intention, the stronger and more effective the appeal is likely to be. Wal-Mart's "to help people save money" does a great job of communicating low price. If the statement does not clearly convey the brand intention, the company has to take steps to assure that, in one form or another, it clearly communicates the customer motivation to the marketplace *and* to its employees. However it is achieved, it's vital that they do it and do it well.

If you intend to create a mission statement or revisit the one you have, look at the mission and purpose statements of companies you admire, companies and businesses that are similar to yours as well as those of your direct competitors. You'll likely find that there are some you like and others you don't. You'll find words and phrases that are attractive to you and others that are not. You'll find some that you can trust and others that you can't.

Other approaches to creating or realigning your mission or vision include a host of Internet sites and services that provide methodologies and best practices for formulating a statement. There are brand consultants who provide resources and processes. Whatever course of action you choose, the result should be to create a statement that best represents your company's aspirations for the future, best conveys your customer motivation and brand intention, and emotionally communicates your vision or mission to the marketplace.

FINDING THE UNIQUE RECIPE

In Chapter Six, we explored the six brand intentions and the definition of a unique recipe. In over twenty years working with and facilitating leaders and teams engaged in visioning and strategic planning, I have found that there are three key impediments to the alignment to brand intention. They appear at the highest levels of leadership and can be found throughout a company. In one form or another, they impede alignment and performance.

The first obstacle occurs when a company's leaders, because of their experiences, do not agree about the brand intention that will best serve the customer. It's not that there are too many chefs in the kitchen. It's that each chef wants to cook his or her favorite dish. While this can often be the case for a new group trying to evaluate and make a decision about what path to customer satisfaction to pursue, it can also affect an experienced group. Often, even with a group of seasoned and experienced leaders, I can be surprised at the level of disconnect and misalignment when it comes to clearly defining what they believe is in the best interest of the customer and the company.

Leaders want to do what they believe is competent and right. That doesn't mean that they will always be in alignment. Typically, the opposite is true. Because each member of a leadership team has his or her own set of experiences, they have different interpretations of what works and what doesn't. After all, if history is a good indication of what will happen and a predictor of future success, it is natural for people to pursue opportunities based on what was successful before. As a result, it's not unusual for each member of the team to try to convince the others that his or her desired direction is the best one.

The second obstacle to alignment is personal preference. As individuals, we all have a natural preference toward one of the three customer motivations and, therefore, will likely favor one brand intention over another. Underlying this is the desire to treat others in the way that we want, and expect, to be treated. For example, one partner in the business has a preference for receiving attention. As a result, he advocates for the brand intention of customization, which aligns to preference. He believes the best way to build the business is to build relationships with customers and offer customized products that the customer is willing to pay more for. Based on his preference, he believes that the best course is to pursue a steady pace of growth while targeting higher margins.

Another member of the team prefers competency and advocates a strategic direction toward low price. Rather than taking a personal approach to the customer, she believes the shopper can be better attracted through discounted pricing. So, she advocates for building the business by gaining market share. She believes it is better to lead customers than be led by them. Because it is more in alignment with her preference for competency and control, she tries to persuade the other team members to pursue the brand intention of low price. She advocates a vision for the company that is anchored in and aligned to quickly building sales volume, taking market share, and operating as efficiently and effectively as possible to maintain lower margins of profitability and win by competing through price.

The purpose of this example is not to advocate for one or the other. It is to provide insight into how easily our preferences are communicated and how easily we allow our preferences, and ultimately our emotions, to guide our thinking and influence our decision-making. Scenarios like this one are fairly common. Depending on a team's or leader's chosen methodology, a group may engage in a competitive analysis, an assessment of market trends and variables, an opportunity and threat analysis, or a number of other processes that allow for the collection and analysis of information to incorporate and guide the strategic planning and decision-making process. Finding the right approach is important. Making certain that everyone involved is aligned to the process is as well. A team can easily find itself in a conversation or debate headed toward an outcome that reflects less of what may be in the shared best interest of the business and more of a contest over whose personal preference comes out on top.

The third obstacle is insecure egos. Every so often members of a team, or the leader, will advocate a direction or make a decision that does not align with what is in the best interest of the business. They want things their way. They may set out to prove that they are the smartest person in the room, regardless of the consequences to the business. They will sometimes set out to prove they can win the argument. It may be the result of a long-standing struggle or conflict with another member or an ongoing debate among multiple members. It can also be the result of partners disagreeing or a long-standing conflict between them. In such instances, other team members can easily disengage, become disinterested, or decide they don't want to participate in the argument and eventually acquiesce. Often, this results in members pursuing their own personal preferences by heading in the direction that delivers the best individual gain and shows little or no concern for alignment.

When leaders or members of a team act out of insecurity, they often abandon the pursuit of alignment and what is in the best interest of the customer. This can create challenges that are difficult to overcome and may cause misalignments that take a long time to recover from and result in time-consuming issues, unnecessary conflict, and dissatisfied customers. Ultimately, a company's success depends on the ability of its leaders to come into alignment and engage the remaining members in the process. As a company grows and expands, its ability to align will be a key influence on its success. To do this effectively, leadership must create a clear vision and strategies that create alignment at the organization and group level. These must then be clearly conveyed and further manifested in the roles, expectations, and goals of every member of the business. Studies show that all too often employees are disengaged and do not feel connected enough to the organization and its vision, strategies, and goals. These are symptoms of misalignment.

ALIGNING STRATEGY

The clarity of and alignment to the brand intention is furthered by the creation, communication, and alignment of vision and strategy. These basic principles, which are essential to success, are the undertakings of leadership, teams and their members.

In brief, *a strategic vision is a clearly articulated description of the desired future state of the company, business, or organization.*

A strategic vision is a powerful means through which we can describe what the enterprise will look like. It provides a clear idea of what is to be achieved and a construct for beginning that keeps the end in mind. Therefore, it can be used to plan the path to achieving that goal. Beyond mission and vision, a strategic perspective helps employees understand what the observable and measurable outcomes are that fulfill its mission and vision. When done well, a strategic vision is compelling. It engages people emotionally and offers a source of motivation.

Strategic visions and organizational strategies are a powerful source of alignment. As a clearly articulated description of the desired future state of the company, business, or organization, strategic visions include a number of key components, one of which is a timeline. For example, a component of the strategic vision of Lands' End is to reach $5 billion. This has a stronger impact if you add the company's timeline—2020. While there is no one approach or formula, a specific set of guidelines for what to include, or standards for the degree of detail, a timeline typically serves a company well.

When the strategic vision is clearly articulated, the next steps are to define the strategies to be undertaken at an organizational level and translate them into aligned group and team strategies. Strategy can be defined in a host of ways. Among them are a plan and a tactical approach to getting things done; a plan for action; a plan for achieving a goal; an approach chosen to bring about a desired future; a method of achieving a goals; a solution to a problem; and, adaptation to change. The common ingredients in most definitions of strategy are plan and change.

My own definition of *strategy is "a plan for change."* After all, strategizing means making decisions about the changes we plan to implement. Strategy is a periodic plan and roadmap, including the clear definition of the changes, outcomes, and goals the company is striving to accomplish, that will enable members of a company or team to realize their mission and vision. The processes we undertake for strategic planning can vary. As we will explore in Chapter Eight, the more aligned the process for strategic planning is to the culture of the business, the greater the level of success in planning, communicating, and executing. The key for success lies in the alignment of the strategy to the mission, vision, and brand intention.

In my experience, strategic vision and strategy has the following five parts. Each is an important ingredient to success and requires alignment.

1. Product and Service Development
2. Market Development
3. Operational Improvement

4. Finance
5. Culture

Product or service development includes the creation and addition of new products or services, diversification, and the improvement and further development of those already being offered. Alignment helps to inform and guide what new products or services best support customer motivation and have a higher likelihood of success and steers them away from those not likely to be attractive to its customers. All too often an idea is generated, moves forward through the process of coming to market, and only then is it discovered that the customer does not see its potential value or connect it to the provider's brand intention.

Cosmopolitan magazine's entry into the yogurt market was an obvious misalignment. As was McDonald's offering of the Arch Deluxe. A few years ago, in an effort to attract new customers, Starbucks began offering a lower priced cup of coffee. The effort failed. The lure of cheaper coffee is out of alignment with the Starbucks brand and isn't about to sway customers loyal to Dunkin Donuts, 7-11, and other low-price sellers.

Depending on the scope of the strategy and the company's size and structure, all elements of development, testing, packaging, and delivery to the customer need to be considered. For products, this includes testing the manufacturing, packaging and distribution, as well as supply-chain elements. All the factors involved in the creation and delivery of the product or service to the customer must be aligned.

Market development vision and strategies include the demographic and geographic considerations of broadening the customer base and selling more of a company's product or service. This includes alignment on what specific segments to target and strategizing on how to penetrate those markets. Several considerations are important to keep in mind. One is how a company may need to adapt to a new market and how the customer may differ from those that the company has had prior success with. Others are the landscape of competition and the pricing levels required.

When a company successfully aligns its market development strategy, it pays attention to all the facets of the customer experience, including brand intention, the various forms of communication, advertising, and packaging. An aligned approach also considers the selling process and what the actual transaction looks and feels like to the customer. In this case, the customer is defined as any person receiving or being affected by your product or service. Even the subtlest forms of influence need to be considered.

Operational improvement strategies are related to the advancement of a company's ability to create and deliver its product or service to the customer. This includes technology, facilities, fleets, equipment, and other elements associated with supply-chain management. While there are a variety of desired outcomes, and the focus of most operational strategies is to improve efficiency and effectiveness, it is always beneficial to remember how operational strategies can quickly come into misalignment with the brand intention and result in performance miscues.

Of the available operational strategies, the one that has been consistent over time is operational excellence. Lean production (aka Lean), just in time (JIT), and Deming's quality movement are all variations and advances on strategies that originated in the scientific management approach created in the early 1890s by Frederick Taylor. Scientific management, Taylor's approach, evolved into industrial efficiency and cost containment. Taylor helped create the assembly line processes that led to the mass production capabilities of the Ford Motor Company. Taylor's basic principles are still incorporated as companies implement strategies focusing on process improvement and systemic thinking to generate sustainable improvements. The end game is successfully implementing changes that preserve customer value with less work.

Financial strategies relate to the analysis and management of a company's monetary goals and objectives. Financial strategies are typically intended to influence three aspects of the company's performance: (1) revenue or the money coming into the company, typically the result of sales: (2) expenses or the money going out of the company; and, (3) profit, or what's left. Of course, it is more complex than that. It also includes decisions on investment strategies and obtaining and using financial resources, implementing controls, tracking and reporting processes, including key performance indicators (KPIs), and managing cash flow and assets.

The alignment of financial strategy is a key lever to success. It includes reporting that enables other parts of the company to be better informed and make better decisions, the support of short-term investment that contributes to long-term outcomes, the management of staffing and hiring priorities, and investment in the advancement of products and services. An essential ingredient of financial strategy is its alignment to the priorities of the company's brand intention, including the investment in creating products or services that respond to the customer motivation.

Without aligning financial strategy to the other strategies a company is undertaking, it is very difficult to make anything happen. It typically results in slowing business and restrains its ability to deliver to the customer and successfully compete in the marketplace.

Culture strategies relate to human resources and the management and leadership of people. I use the term culture in lieu of human resources, people, or human capital to highlight a more systemic approach to what is ultimately the most important of the five company strategies. I can't stress enough the impact of human resource and organizational development strategies and initiatives on the alignment and the culture of a company, as well as on what the company does and how it creates and delivers its products or services to its customers. While well intended, too often strategies and approaches that appear attractive or cutting edge don't align to the company's culture, causing misalignment and confusion.

Along with recruiting and hiring practices, a company's culture includes compensation and reward, teaming practices, organizational structure, leadership development, training and development, personnel practices, payroll and employee policy administration, and employee engagement. In Chapter Eight, we'll take a closer look at the definition of culture and the characteristics that can be applied in alignment to the brand intention and a company's other strategies. Leaders of companies large and small have realized the importance of taking a more strategic view of intentionally leading culture through clear communication of the company's values and beliefs and hiring people based on how well they fit the culture. In initially creating your strategic vision, every facet may carry different weight, yet touching on each provides you the ability to later create a more specific set of action items with more specific timeframes, quantifiable definitions, and measurements of success, including the responsibilities of each department and member of the team.

Once the strategic vision and company strategies are defined and aligned at the organizational level, the next step is aligning them for each part of the business. This may include multiple locations, divisions, units, teams and groups. Often, different parts of the organization or individuals, in light of their narrow focus, can easily fall into misalignment. One characteristic of great leaders and their organizations is constant attention to coaching each individual. This is true for large global competitors, small-to medium-size businesses, and local and family businesses. Business is a human art, requiring the ongoing development and alignment of the people in the business.

FPS COMPANY

To illustrate how to apply the five parts of strategy and how important the ongoing conversation about alignment is, let's examine a hypothetical small company that wants to grow. The aspects of alignment and the challenges it faces apply to any size company.

As you read, try to identify the various strategic implications the FPS Company will face and what strategic considerations and alignment opportunities the leadership will to have to address. It helps to make lists that reflect the five parts: product or service development, market development, operational improvement, finance, and culture.

The FPS Company builds and sells high-quality playground equipment to schools, cities, and communities. The company's mission is "To be the leading provider of high-quality playground equipment." Over the past two decades, it has built a reputation for innovative approaches to construction, superior designs, and timely delivery. It is considered the preeminent brand by experts and its competitors. It successfully sells higher priced, quality playground equipment that others attempt to replicate.

In support of its vision and desire to grow, its leadership has decided to expand its customer base and leverage the products or services it offers. In exploring ways to accomplish this, the CEO and her team decide to introduce a select line to the consumer market. While the company's current customers are primarily school districts and city park departments, the team believes the consumer market offers an excellent opportunity. The company adopts a longer term strategic vision to successfully penetrate that market. The goal is to profitably generate revenue of at least $5 million by the end of the first three years after entering the consumer market. Based on its findings, the leadership team believes that the company can eventually become a strong niche player in a multibillion dollar global market.

Starting with the end in mind, the FPS Company's leadership team begins by identifying the different elements required by its new direction. It creates a list of key outcomes and defines the actions, measurable outcomes, and timelines required to attain success. The leaders clearly define what is needed to fulfill its strategic vision, create an aligned organizational level strategy, and formulate a plan that includes each of the elements required for success.

From a product or service standpoint, the majority of the products they plan to offer are already part of their current product line and bundled offerings, yet decisions are needed about which products will likely perform best and how they will be priced to meet the profit margins targeted. This requires additional market research into what successes and failures the consumer side competitors have experienced and what can be learned from them. While the company's sales and service processes are very successful working with schools, park departments, and townships, it will need to find ways to sell and deliver to consumers townships. Among other factors, this includes the skills required to sell to this new set of buyers, how to brand itself in the new market, how to create new paths for its marketing, and how to best reach and sell to its new customers.

One of the realities the company faces is that consumer knowledge of its current brand, FPS Company, is very limited, and a number of competitors, although selling lesser quality and lower-priced playground equipment, have well-established brand presence in the marketplace. Several of these lower priced competitors have well-developed channels for selling, including relationships with the big box stores like Home Depot, Wal-Mart, and Lowes. The FPS team is not only faced with identifying what its sales channel options are, it must determine what its most effective marketing and selling approaches will be and how to service its new customers, particularly since the company's practices need to be adjusted to the consumer market.

Depending on what route FPS takes in selling to the consumer market, it needs to create new packaging and ways to deliver its products. It will need to design and execute new processes suited to the specific line of products it intends to sell to this market, as well as adjust and possibly reorganize its inventory and supply-chain practices. Whether it will be selling through retailers or going direct to consumers, logistics must be put in place for shipping and delivering.

Based on projections, and taking a longer term view, FPS may need to consider adding additional manufacturing capability. Along with added manpower, it may require other, more specially designed equipment. And, while there may be pricing advantages the company can gain from purchasing larger quantities of raw materials and product components, there will be logistical changes needed to store, handle, and effectively manage the additional inventory.

Operationally, the team will also need to consider the additional information technology capability required, which will include an assessment of what will have to be added to, or leveraged from, its enterprise system and how this new aspect will be integrated into its business.

All these strategic challenges will need to be reflected in FPS's financial planning process. This includes budgeting for the various aspects of the company's expansion, as well as defining and integrating the new tracking and reporting requirements for the new consumer side of the business. It will certainly require a close examination of how to manage the risks associated with entering the consumer market, including the possible new requirements for product liability insurance. Each strategic aspect of product or service development, market development, and operational improvement will need to be considered, along with estimates for additional staffing and competency requirements. The need for sound financial strategies and practices become obvious.

Last, the management team will need to explore how it will lead and guide the company through the changes necessary for success. This will require the ongoing alignment of its human resource practices and strategies to its culture and the multiple aspects of the organizational strategy. This includes how it will, through its expansion and growth, sustain and further develop its culture and assure that the company's core values and beliefs are apparent in how it strategically executes. This affects how it recruits and hires talent, incents and rewards its people, and creates an environment that engages employees to be innovative and motivated to perform their best, as well as how it develops the leaders required to successfully take and grow the company.

At the outset of the FPS Company story, I asked you to track the strategic challenges and alignment opportunities. You were probably able to identify many. Without going into great detail, the FPS leadership team and the company's employees have quite an undertaking before them— a set of challenges that require a great deal of alignment among the members of the management team, the various parts of the business, and every person in the company. One of the more obvious requirements for the extraordinary performance of any company is for its leaders (every one of them) to get aligned and committed to contributing to the company's vision, mission, and brand intention, because misalignment at the top creates the "us versus them" conflicts that lead to the all-too-common dysfunctions that result in the breakdown of teamwork and collaboration necessary for success. Differences among leaders or partners are played out between the coalitions of team members and employees who join in the quarrels and end up creating more misalignments throughout the company.

Therefore, before embarking on the creation and alignment of strategy at the organizational or company level, it is imperative that the leadership first attains alignment to mission, vision, and brand intention. Misalignment occurs most frequently when a company is pursuing new market initiatives or finds itself in the throes of change.

CONFRONTING SILOS, STOVEPIPES, AND OTHER MISALIGNMENTS

When it comes to overcoming the misalignments of teams and groups, the most powerful thing you can do is focus everyone on alignment.

Returning to the FPS Company, let's fast forward a year. The leadership team decided to pursue the retail consumer strategy and put a great deal of effort and resources behind it. Based on market data and competitive analysis, the company decided to introduce a new consumer brand to the marketplace. Using the company's original name of Fun Play Stuff (FPS), it decided to enter the market as a higher quality alternative and carve out a customer niche that would separate it from the host of lower priced offerings. The company committed to building a brand reputation through retail sellers and to develop an Internet and print-based advertising approach. Of these two approaches, the marketing team was unsure which would provide the best course for the future.

Parallel to the development of the Internet-based selling strategy, implementation of which was in the hands of the small IT group, the marketing and sales team began implementing its strategy to sell to retailers. In the past, the company's sales team had relied on its ability to build relationships with individual school districts, local governments, and communities. A big part of the company's successful entry into the consumer market would depend on its ability to develop a sales force that could sell differently, even as they wanted to be sure FPS continues its mission "To be the leading provider of high-quality playground equipment" and keep its aligned preeminent pricing strategy.

As part of its operational strategy, the leadership team decided to increase production and create an inventory of the select set of products its market data demonstrated would be most likely to sell. In product design and manufacturing, the company has always held itself to an unwavering commitment to making and delivering only products of the highest quality. In design and manufacturing, the thinking was that maintaining the company's very demanding quality and safety specifications was the key to success. As manufacturing expanded its capabilities and began to slowly increase production and inventory, the group focused on assuring that its new production capabilities aligned to this most important of company values.

Meanwhile, in marketing and sales and in pursuit of the new retail market, FPS hired a small team of sales professionals with strong backgrounds and expertise selling to retailers. As soon as they made their first sales calls, the feedback was that FPS had to offer products at a more competitive pricing level. Many of these salespeople had achieved success selling based on competitive pricing and working with retailers to create attractive customer offerings. Faced with the choice of selling based on quality or price, they accepted the feedback and promised their customers that they would return with more competitively priced offerings.

Confronted with price conscious retailers and wanting to offer a high-quality and safe product, the design and manufacturing groups pushed back. They argued that it wasn't a matter of price. Their perception was that the new salespeople did not understand and were therefore unable to communicate and sell the value of FPS's higher quality equipment. The design team also took the long-term view that once the website was up and running and the planned social media campaign took hold, the resulting sales would prove their position. After all, the brand had been built on the company's relentless pursuit of quality and safety.

In the meantime, following the lead of the design team and the original sales projections provided by the marketing and sales team, manufacturing continued to ramp up and slowly build the company's new product inventory. It came as a surprise when they heard that the marketing and sales group wanted products for the retail market that could be sold at a lower price. Not convinced of this new strategy, the design and manufacturing groups, who were happy making superior products, did not consider delivering a new lower priced line a priority and displayed no sense of urgency creating it.

As a result, the sales team became discouraged. Blaming the product design team for dragging its feet, the sales team began pointing fingers at design and manufacturing for not responding to the customer's needs. They began to question where leadership was on this one. The marketing leader seemed to be at odds with the design team leader, while the leader in manufacturing was becoming concerned about the inventory buildup and the costs associated with it. He openly began questioning whether anyone was clear about what now appeared to be a very misaligned set of group and team strategies. He pointed out that all of this would be very costly and possibly catastrophic, and he wondered whether to stop manufacturing certain products and possibly reduce his employee headcount.

Eventually, FPS was forced to confront its misalignments and refocus its efforts in pursuit of an aligned organizational level strategy. It wasn't easy. The company's CEO had to confront individual team members and engage the team in constructively collaborating to overcome its misalignments. By focusing on creating alignment, the team identified and problem solved its misalignments. Team members took individual and shared responsibility for creating an urgent approach to realigning the company. It began by reaffirming its values and beliefs and reinforcing its preeminent brand position.

In an effort to protect its quality brand, it devised a strategy to sell through the relationships it already enjoyed and could readily expand. It targeted consumers in specific markets, including the cities and municipalities where it already enjoyed success, and began targeting the income demographic associated with the school districts already familiar with the product and brand. At the individual level, each member of the marketing and sales team was trained and coached so that they would be empowered, at any moment and in any situation, to manage customers in alignment to the company's brand intention and values. The company coordinated these efforts with a broad social media campaign engaging its target audience with entertaining videos and exciting forms of local crowd sourcing campaigns. The company's website was soon offering emotionally charged images of happy children and parents, playing fearlessly and freely, and demonstrating full trust in the quality and reliability of FPS products. The adjustments to its manufacturing and inventory targets, while at times painful to execute, realigned levels of production output and inventory. The design team, taking customer feedback and striving to be innovative, began producing new and more attractive consumer products and further leveraging its new designs in the parks, schools, and community product lines. Soon, the company's Internet-focused marketing and selling took hold, resulting in additional school districts, municipalities, and communities buying into FPS as the preferred brand choice for their playgrounds and parks. FPS had found its path to building and enjoying its reputation as the niche provider of the highest quality safe consumer play equipment, strengthening the power of its brand by further separating itself from its competition.

While this storybook ending may seem a bit much, it's not an unlikely tale. Think about G. Hensler. On a much larger scale, IBM offers an extremely powerful example of a company pursuing misaligned strategies and finding its way back to becoming an aligned global powerhouse. And, how many remember that Apple was once struggling to stay alive. Eventually, it realigned itself and, with a relentless commitment to innovative technology and preeminent approaches to retailing, found success. (What isn't often seen by most of its customers is its behind-the-scenes operational alignment, which exhibits the same level of innovation as its products.)

In 2004, Lego was limping along and close to $1billion in debt as a result of creating a large number of products and losing focus. It drastically reduced the number of product offerings and became very focused on being more select and aligned to the almost collector-like behavior of its customers. Its realignment is one of the greatest comeback stories in any industry. At the outset of 2013, Lego was the highest valued toy company in the world.

Many of us are familiar with the Old Spice Man. In 2010, videos of the reinvented champion of the brand leisurely sitting atop his white stallion went viral. Yet if you look at the brand's history, you would quickly discover the modern version of the icon brand is merely an updated and aligned version of a character that baby boomers know from the early 1970s. The message of charisma, quirkiness, and good scent plays just as well today as it did decades ago. With it came the reinvigoration of a brand almost forgotten.

The tale of the FPS Company demonstrates how easily a company or team can become misaligned. It also shows us, as the other real examples do, that a misaligned company or team can work its way back into alignment. The story also reminds us that when misaligned, the first step to recovery is confronting what is happening. The alignment framework provides a powerful means to confront misalignments and offers a shared lens and language that members of a team or company can use to collaborate and problem solve instead of getting bogged down in endless arguments and blaming one another. A shared understanding and framework gives a group the structure it often desperately needs to focus on the actual issues and problems.

TRUST IN THE FRAMEWORK

Is it often said that if one trusts in the process, the intended outcome will be reached. More often than not this proves to be true. Trusting the process can be difficult. Many distractions and forces can take you off course and change your focus. Yet, if you stay on course, the framework for alignment will provide a basis for accomplishing most of what a company or team needs to reach higher levels of performance and achievement.

The elements of alignment provide a framework that can be used as a step-by-step process, and you can leverage any part of it to focus on the issue at hand. That approach serves us well, yet can limit our thinking, our perceived choices, and our actions. At times, adherence to step-by-step processes can make us rigid, which doesn't serve us well.

Frequently, our models for teams and companies apply strategic thinking periodically. In the end, success requires both processes for planning *and* structures for the ongoing assessment and confrontation of the issues and challenges of misalignment. I encourage you to use the framework as a process for strategic alignment *and* as the basis for ongoing conversation.

Before going forward, let's briefly review the framework.

Begin with the end in mind. The first step is to clearly articulate the company's mission and purpose, thereby communicating why the company exists. It always begins with the customer.

Brand Intention. To succeed, a business must be able to explain why the customer is spending money for a product or service with one company over another. Brand intention is the thoughtful and deliberate delivery, through a product or service, of your promise to the customer. It goes beyond statements of a customer or brand promise, market differentiator, and competitive advantage, which are aspects of brand intention.

Vision. The vision of a company provides a clearly articulated picture of the future. It includes five key parts: product and service development, market development, operational improvement, finance, and culture. The vision communicates what a company is intended to look like.

Strategy. A company's strategy provides the plan for change that is communicated to employees. The strategy clearly defines measurable goals and outcomes, provides timelines, and explains how the goals will be achieved. It also establishes the company's strategic priorities and aligns shorter term initiatives to longer term outcomes and assigns responsibility to the various parts and individuals.

Group and Team Strategy. Each part of a company must know and understand how its performance contributes to the successful delivery of the product or service to the customer. In alignment to the company strategy, group and team strategies provide a detailed periodic that clearly defines the measurable goals and outcomes, the timelines, and how the strategic outcomes of the team will be achieved. In alignment to the company's brand intention and strategy, a team's strategy will also align to the company's strategic priorities. It also assigns roles and responsibilities to the various members of the team.

Personal Goals and Development. Individual responsibilities are defined and, to further individual engagement, are aligned to the group and company strategies. This includes measurable and well-defined outcomes, clearly articulated authority for decision making, and expectations for the individual's contribution to team or group priorities and performance. In high-performing teams and groups, the opportunity for the development of each individual member is incorporated.

Thus, I've focused on providing a framework for aligning the what and the why of business. Now, we'll turn our attention to the first step in aligning culture—defining it.

EIGHT

Decoding Culture

How do things really get done?

Before becoming a leadership and organizational psychologist, I enjoyed a career as a chef and restaurateur. Before that, I was a casualty
lines underwriter. I was hired right out of high school as a trainee by a
large insurance firm and eventually landed at a small high-risk underwriting group. After a successful seven-year run, I decided it was not
for me. I had always had an interest in the culinary arts and, while still at
the underwriting firm, I began working part time as a line cook, which
reignited my love of cooking. I resigned and moved to Hyde Park, New
York, to attend the Culinary Institute of America.

Upon graduation, I received a number of offers, including one from
the Galway Cooking School in Ireland, one from La Récolte, a top-rated
restaurant in New York City, and another to spend two years as a sous
chef at a luxury resort in Switzerland. My wife and I had just our first
child and, choosing to stay close to our families, I accepted the offer from
La Récolte, which had been ranked number four on *New York Magazine*'s
top restaurant list. The restaurant's executive chef, Jean-Marie Pougnet,
had been recruited from a Michelin-starred restaurant in France, was
in his late twenties, and was already considered one of France's top young
chefs. At La Récolte, he had assembled an incredibly talented group of
chefs, and I was honored to be joining them.

None of my experiences prepared me for La Récolte. The ambiance was enticingly warm and welcoming, yet impeccably arranged, meticulously organized, and subtly luxurious. The cleanliness and organization was readily apparent at the back of the house and the kitchen. The chefs preparing for the evening's dinner service were calmly going about their work with a fluidity I had never seen. I was greeted by Jean-Marie. His appearance was flawless. After a brief tour, Jean-Marie chuckled, and asked in his thick French accent, "So Edgaah, how do yuh like zee keetchen?"

"It looks great. I like it a great deal." I replied. "And it smells really good."

Jean-Marie gave me a terse look. "Food dose not smell Edgaah! It az en errr-oma. It az a beautee-ful errroma."

Welcome to the culture of La Récolte. Stepping onto the cooking line was intimidating. Not only would a mistake by one of the line chefs be a costly error, imperfection was simply not tolerated. As a chef at La Récolte, you were expected to always be at your best, to always perform under pressure, and do it in a calm, consistent, and confident manner. To move forward in the ranks, not only did you have to demonstrate competence, you also had to be innovative, and creative, with an in-depth knowledge of wine and cuisine and a refined palate.

The expected high level of quality and performance was apparent in everything, even if the customer would never see it. To be untidy, unshaven, or not look the part of the chef was unacceptable. There was no formal code. Yet everyone adhered to the same set of standards. There were other aspects of the restaurant's culture that defined the tradition of La Récolte. Chef's table was one of them. Jean-Marie orchestrated the timing of this afternoon ritual. Everyone was expected to stop what he or she was doing and sit down to break bread together. I found this out during my first week in the kitchen, when I fell a bit behind in my preparation for dinner service and unknowingly made the choice to continue my work. Not being prepared to take time for chef's table was not an acceptable choice. Not only was it considered rude; it was an indication that you were disorganized or not sufficiently competent. Luckily, during one of my first weeks, one of the other chefs took me aside and explained the importance of participating. The exchange did not go unnoticed by Jean-Marie, who made it a point to reinforce that I had made the right decision by explaining that chef's table was part of the bond and camara-derie we all enjoyed and what made us special.

In the kitchen at La Récolte, there were no signs containing mission statements, values and beliefs, or rules to guide behavior. You had to dis-cover how to fit into the culture by recognizing its nuances, gathering information, and asking questions. There was no formal orientation. You had to be a quick study.

MOVING BEYOND TRIAL AND ERROR

Entering and becoming a member of a new culture is not unusual, whether it's a new workgroup or a new team or a new job. Discovering how to successfully become a new member of an existing group is typically our first priority. "Fitting in" is a key part of our shared human experience and a crucial part of any group's culture. All people want to feel safe; to be free from the fear of being ignored, humiliated, ostracized, unloved, rejected, embarrassed, feeling like a loser. When we are not afraid, we feel secure, confident to be ourselves, and act authentically in the manner that reflects what we think, see, and feel.

Until we understand the culture of a company or team, we constantly risk saying or doing something that offends our coworkers. Typically, when first thinking about how a product or service is created and deliv-ered to the customer, we first describe our activities, including the meth-ods, procedures, and systems. Sometimes, we explain the performance of our roles and tasks and the approaches and means by which our out-comes are achieved. In technical and mechanical environments, we might discuss our use of technology, equipment, or devices. We might also mention the knowledge, skills, and competencies required, the results we achieve, and the level of performance to which we aspire.

All of these are important aspects of how we get things done. Yet, a deeper, more meaningful aspect of the *how* influences the way in which people contribute to their groups, teams, and companies.

Culture guides how we behave toward and work with one another; it dictates whether a company or team reaches its true potential. It is why culture is a key lever in attaining alignment.

Just as intention defines the *what* and *why* of business, culture defines the *how*. The definition of culture goes beyond describing the processes, procedures, and systems we use to create and deliver a product or service; it describes the richness and depth of how the members of an organization or team interact.

It is important to remember that business is a human art. Our motivations connect us as customers, as members of teams and groups, and as individuals within organizations and their cultures. No matter the size of the group, culture is the result of how people work together and get done things. Culture guides and influences how each member behaves and expresses his or her motivations and desires. Our behaviors and interactions take on patterns that eventually result in what are called *cultural norms*. Underlying them are layers of values, shared meaning, belief systems, paradigms, philosophies, and assumptions.

A SIMPLE DEFINITION

Unfortunately, most leaders do not do a very good job of directing their cultures in a purposeful and effective manner. This is not from a lack of interest or desire for a strong and healthy culture. Rather, it is because they lack a framework for creating a sound vision and strategy for their cultures. Leaders typically create and develop a culture through trial and error.

When it comes to strategic thinking, culture rarely gets the attention it deserves, and leaders are seldom taught about culture or explore it in any depth. It is usually not thought about until a contentious issue or conflict arises, and it becomes a problem. Then, it is often viewed as politics: clashing coalitions with differing ideals seeking power and influence to win over an individual, group, or inner circle because influencing them will result in resources, perks, and perceived favoritism. It's rare to find a company of size that does not have a preferred circle or hierarchy through which individuals attain increased influence. This is not always a negative; it depends on how it is used and how it impacts the rest of the company. When it has a negative influence, such maneuvering for the right to dictate or control direction, it is typically an indication of misalignment.

Unfortunately, leaders and managers are given only the definition of values and beliefs through which to define culture. They are not taught how to reinforce them effectively. Without a measurable and observable framework, leaders are left to figure it out for themselves, and individuals must come to terms with what is expected of them. In this chapter, I will provide a comprehensive framework that will enable you to understand the power of culture. I will also give you a common language and set of principles for observing and measuring culture that can be applied strategically in alignment to the business's brand intention. A strong culture that doesn't align to brand intention can be as damaging as a weak one.

Among others, Peter Drucker, Warren Bennis, Peter Senge, John Kotter and James Heskett, William Schneider, Jon Katzenbach, Jerry Parros, and Jim Collins have all weighed in on the definition of culture. Each offers a unique perspective on, and definition of, culture. They also have much in common.

Culture defines how people individually and collectively interact with one another to get things done. This includes how they create success for themselves and one another, and what is acceptable and unacceptable behavior. Every company, team, and group has a unique culture.

Culture is like personality. We can readily identify particular behaviors and associate them with styles and personal traits. The resulting patterns that emerge define who we are. There is no one formula for a successful culture. For example, a rock band's tour bus differs greatly from a children's school bus. Both achieve the desired outcome of arriving at their destinations on time; they just go about it in very different ways. The behavior requirements for riders on a band's tour bus and passengers on a school bus are vastly different. Similarly, as we define culture and describe its consistent and characteristics, remember that there are nuances of behavior and interaction in each organization or team and how it operates that make them different from one another.

Words that describe values and beliefs (i.e., respect, integrity, quality, trust, and teamwork) do not themselves adequately define a culture. It is the interaction of human beings that allows the language of a particular culture to take on and express their true meaning. For example, if I were to ask a group of fifteen leaders to write a one sentence definition of what the word integrity means in their company's culture, I'd likely get a diverse set of definitions.

Culture keys—the many characteristics that define culture—are the strategic levers that bring into being and help define the emotional forces that influence behavior. They can be applied to strategically influence the culture to manifest the preferred patterns of individual and group behavior. They can also be used to better and more clearly articulate how the culture is to be aligned. The culture keys also provide a set of observable and often measurable characteristics, which help to clearly articulate and communicate them.

One culture key, for instance, is the interpretation of how decisions are made. Often, groups lack clarity about what decisions are needed, what conversations leading to the decision should look like, who is involved, what level of participation is required or expected, who has the final say, and who is responsible for communicating and implementing the decision. By articulating and defining the decision-making process, we can better observe and manage how it is used in planning, in problem solving, and in generating, sharing, and using information. This is why the alignment of power and influence, and whether it is used intentionally or unintentionally, usually originates from the leader.

Among other characteristics of behavior, culture provides insight into the level and quality of communication and interaction among the members and parts of an organization. One of the most valuable is how conflict is managed and resolved. In fact, an individual's first experience, and the one through which that person will interpret the culture, occurs when he or she first observes or engages in a conflict. The level of collaboration or win-lose posturing provides a great deal of information about what conflicts to engage in, the appropriate level of participation, and whether to argue or fall in line. How members respond is an aspect of what is acceptable and unacceptable behavior.

Strategically, culture keys include how members are empowered and rewarded, how compensation and promotion is used, how hiring occurs, and what the focus of employee development is. Culture offers insight into how teams are created and defines cooperation, collaboration, and how people challenge one another. When individuals do not act responsibly, culture also explains how they hold one another accountable. Leaders must realize that culture keys provide a powerful strategic approach to how the team or company can be purposely aligned with the experience of the customer. The greater the alignment of a culture's internal behaviors to the external expectation and experience of the customer, the greater the trust in the product or service, the people delivering it, and the brand.

THE CULTURE KEYS

When a guitar maker builds a new instrument, he or she starts with a plan and a template of how the new guitar will look. The first and foremost consideration is how the instrument will be used, which affects the type, shape, and size of the guitar. The parts are pretty much the same for all guitars, yet, if it's an electric guitar, it requires pick-ups and a jack. Other options include a choice of wood and materials to be used, whether a pick guard is needed, and what color and finish is to be applied.

When the guitar is maker is finished, two very important steps remain to be taken. The first is the addition of strings, without which the guitar has no musical value. The second is to tune the strings to the desired pitch.

Once the instrument is played, the strings stretch and wear, requiring the player to repeatedly fine tune the guitar. Occasionally, strings will need to be replaced. The guitar will also undergo wear and tear, requiring maintenance and repair. The more it is played, the more it will open up; that is, its tone and resonance will develop, and the guitar will sound richer, making it more valuable to the player. The better it gets, the more players will be interested in playing it, and it will likely increase in value. Nevertheless, most of its parts will remain the same. However, each player will influence its tuning—the alignment of the strings to create tone and harmony.

Building and leading the culture of an extraordinary company is much like building and playing a great instrument. While the basic ingredients are the same, what the business does will affect specific aspects of how it is designed and built. Pragmatic decisions will be made reflecting the practical considerations of size, structure, and the systems needed to support its functions and processes. The way a business meets the demands of how it is intended to perform and how it will attract customers and resonate in the marketplace must be defined. Just as a guitar needs a player, the company needs talented and creative people to bring it to life, and, like a guitar, constant attention is required to bring it into alignment. The leader must know how to tune the keys.

Over time, a company will need to be looked after, maintained and, occasionally, repaired. A leader must take pride in and constantly look after the health and well- being of a company's culture so that regardless of who leads it in the future, it will be a prized instrument on which the art of business is played.

Guitars now typically have six to twelve tuning keys, while older versions had four. Variations of the guitar include the simpler 3-string Turkish baglama, the 4- and 5-string banjo, and the more complex 20-string sitar. Like these instruments, a company can be highly intricate and contain more keys; the more intricate and the more complex a company is, the more demanding and challenging the alignment may be. For this reason, we will focus on the keys to alignment that have a great effect on culture and will provide you with the greatest leverage. As you read, consider which of the culture keys you already strategically apply, as well as those that offer a new opportunity to create further alignment. Second, explore how they are presently being used, the influence they currently have on your culture, and what opportunities you have to leverage them further. Third, as you identify each culture key you currently apply, begin thinking about whether it is aligned or misaligned to the company culture. Last, remember that values and beliefs are words that can be understood in different ways and be subject to personal interpretation. Try to further articulated them with clarity and provide specific meanings that align them to your particular culture.

Key #1: Power and Influence

Power and influence is a major contributor to what is known as the politics of the culture. They also provide insight into how leaders affect the activities and actions of the team or company. Historically, there are three sources of human motivation. In some cultures, the source of individual and team power lies in the expertise, knowledge, experience, and competency associated with a person or persons. This may also be reflected in the level of authority granted to someone through a title or rank (i.e., team leader, project owner, practice leader). Such power can sometimes be further leveraged by taking control of situations that offer the opportunity to reinforce one's capability, know-how, or proficiency. In other instances, amiability and friendliness is the source of power and influence, reflecting the human motivation of attention and conveyance of importance and significance. In some cultures, encouraging and inviting others to participate is a means to engage influence; listening and creating mutual respect transmit recognizable power. A level of social interaction exists in all teams and companies that can be leveraged as influence. In some cultures, the more socially active one is, the greater the impact one may have on others.

A third distinctive source of influence and power results when individuals are seen as truthful, genuine and forthright, and as acting out of a commitment to a set of higher values and beliefs. Often, individuals who are transparent and are aligned with a set of values and ideals that fit with those of the culture attain great personal power. While it can easily be overlooked, this source of influence often results in informal leadership that, despite an individual not having a formal title, rank, or position of granted authority, manifests significant power.

Key #2: Planning and Goal Setting

Planning and goal-setting processes typically have the same primary steps and components. For example, once a mission and vision are articulated, most strategic planning processes have similar elements of market and competitor analysis, assessment of the company's strengths and weaknesses, identification of opportunities and threats, articulation of organizational and group strategies, and so on. What varies from culture to culture is how they are used. This is an important point because *the principles that are applied to the alignment of how planning and goal setting are undertaken apply to the alignment of the practices associated with leading change.* When we think about strategy, we think about planning. When we think about planning, we think about change. Strategy is a plan for change.

When we look at planning through the lens of change, we realize the significance of aligning planning processes to the culture. One thing that makes the alignment of the approach to planning to culture so powerful is the consistency it provides. When people undergo change, they go through a period of transition during which they may experience fear of the unknown and worry about how it will affect them. The result may be denial and resistance as they grapple with whatever they may have to relinquish. For this reason, consistency, which takes the form of culture, is essential.

In this case, consistency relates to how things get done. When people are asked to participate in a familiar way in a strategy for change, it provides an emotional anchor from which to plan and contribute to setting goals. Thus, if leaders of a company with a collaborative culture of high involvement invite employees to contribute to planning, it represents a welcome opportunity and makes the change more acceptable. It is consistent with the experience of the employees and their perception of the culture. If a plan and directives are handed down without their involvement, they will likely respond emotionally and act with a greater sense of fear and anxiety.

The opposite can also happen when a culture is more authoritarian, and plans for change are cascaded from the top with little employee involvement. Employees expect to be told what to do; their goals and performance expectations are provided to them. If they are accustomed to this culture and have relied on it for personal success, they are likely to trust and execute the leadership's plan. If they are asked to participate and be more involved, they may not know how to engage and may not trust a process that is out of alignment with how things typically are done.

A variety of approaches to planning and goal setting directly impact how successful the outcomes are, including:

- How the process aligns to the values and beliefs of the culture.
- The breadth and depth of involvement.
- The use of analytic and assessment tools.
- The required level of expertise.
- The use of tools that align to the culture.
- The definitions of empowerment.
- The common goals across the company.
- How time efficient or organic it is.

How schedules and milestones for team and individual performance and accomplishments are set and managed are also important considerations, as is how projects are managed. This includes how resources are managed in support of projects and programs, because they can often come into misalignment and result in project delays and cost overruns, thereby creating the possibility of failure. It is important to recognize how to best align planning and goal setting, as well as change management, to culture, since misalignment can impede necessary change and be very costly. When it comes to aligning for change, one can never fine tune enough.

Key #3: Problem Solving

All of the culture keys play a significant role in defining and articulating aspects of culture and affect how people are influenced. A group's lack of understanding about how a problem is to be solved or a decision is to reached can have significant consequences. The reason is that the process for problem solving is not only a platform for power and influence, it also affects how individuals relate to their own motivations to be heard, to be competent, and to decide how open and honest they can afford to be.

When it comes to the various approaches and the definitions of problem solving and decision making, there is ample room for misinterpretation, confusion, and mistrust. This can result in a lack of commitment not only to the identification and creation of possible solutions, yet also to the level of employee commitment and buy-in to the implementation of the outcome.

When the process for problem solving is unclear, members of a team or group may not engage and participate. Because all the necessary information is not brought into the process, the best possible solutions and options will not be manifested. There can be varying degrees of lack of participation, yet even if it is minimal, the person with the most important information or data may not be heard or the person with the best possible idea or insight may not share it with the group. Assuring that every person is involved in the problem solving process is always a good idea.

Different processes and approaches work well for certain cultures, and it is important to find and use those that align best. A good example of an often-used approach to problem solving that requires clear alignment is brainstorming. While there are a many definitions and step-by-step processes for brainstorming, the only approach that will really work is one that aligns to the culture of the group. For example, two requirements of brainstorming that are consistently included are (1) staying with the process until all ideas are generated by the members of the group (often referred to as working to exhaustion) and (2) refraining from making judgmental statements or critiquing ideas until input from all members of the group are heard and recorded.

Sometimes these two requirements align to the culture of the group (Group A), and members easily commit to and engage each other in this way. The group believes that the path to successfully developing the best solutions is based on everyone participating and being heard, getting the greatest number of ideas to work with, and collaborating to find the best idea or combination of ideas to address the problem. Another group's culture (Group B) places greater value on the members of the group challenging one another. Its version of brainstorming is less about everyone being involved and more about those with the best ideas stepping forward and getting involved. It's less about getting as many ideas as possible as it is about finding the quickest path to the best solution.

Groups A's approach is not better than Group B's. What is important is that each group engages in a brainstorming process that best aligns to its culture and how it gets results. This insight helps us determine a number of factors that influence how members of a team or company engage in solving problems and tackle its challenges. Among those to be considered are alignment on the desired results; the expectations for participation in problem solving; the process that will be applied; how information and data are used and developed, including the specific roles that are undertaken as part of fact and data; and the definitions of collaboration. Numerous tools and processes can be applied to problem solving; in all cases, the process will be smoother if those involved are clear on all of them and if the methods feel familiar and reflect the culture of the group and how it really goes about doing things.

Key #4: Decision Making

A major source of predictability and strength in a culture comes from clearly defined roles, as well as the responsibility and authority people have to make decisions. Lack of clarity and alignment on how decisions are made is one of the major sources of conflict. A host of considerations surround process, participation, and empowerment. All cultures require clear definitions of the level of authority that individual and groups have to make decisions and how this affects the results.

Decisions can be made by a single person, by an influential minority, by majority vote, and by consensus. The key is not always which is used; it is often the clarity and understanding of how it is defined and how consistently it is applied. While not everyone will agree with how decisions are made, the process should at least be predictable. When it is unclear, misunderstood, or inconsistent, it often results in conflict, disagreement, and further misalignment.

Many leaders say they expect other members of the team to participate; that, as leaders, they take a participative approach and involve others in the process. Before proceeding, however, look at your own preference and your definition of participative decision making. Then, continue reading.

Every leader has a unique perspective and approach to decision making. Some bring issues to the team and ask members to share their perspectives and collaborate on reaching a consensus decision. Such leaders believe their role is to encourage the team's collaboration and best serve the team by supporting its outcome.

Others gather the team members and ask them to participate in the decision. The team provides its insights and perspectives. The leader listens to their input, takes it under advisement, and then makes his or her decision. Some leaders will have already made a decision, yet they will still ask team members for their opinions to give everyone a sense of involvement and get their buy in.

Thus, the definition of participative decision making can differ from culture to culture, leader to leader, and team member to team member. For this reason, it is important to always be clear about what the approach is. The following is a short list of options:

Single-Person: One person—often the leader or someone appointed the leader or group or a person with the defined role—is given the responsibility and authority to make the decision. Influence can also originate from expertise, relationships, connectivity, and authenticity.

Minority: Whether the group consists of two, three, or more, minority decisions are made by a group that represents a minority of the whole. This typically occurs in two ways. First, the leader gives a small group or team the authority to make a decision. The second is when a small group influences the larger group to agree with its conclusion. A minority group may also be granted authority by a larger group based on the individual or collective competence or roles of its members.

Majority:	The majority comes to a conclusion that becomes the group decision. Sometimes, as is the case of a board of directors, a formal vote is taken; the position receiving the most votes becomes the group's decision. More often, informal processes for measuring the majority are used.
Consensus:	This approach typically requires the most clarification, so a good definition of consensus should be articulated. A consensus decision requires the collaboration of those involved. In most instances, teams and groups use consensus to encourage individuals to be innovative and creative in finding the best possible outcome. Too often, despite good intentions, the group uses one of the previously mentioned approaches; and the idea of consensus is used to solicit the "buy-in" of individual members, who do not agree with the decision. A popular approach is to ask everyone, regardless of their position on the issue, to support the group decision. Note, however, that a big difference will be seen in the behavior and contribution of group members who are committed to the decision and action and those who are merely showing their buy-in or acting out of compliance.
Unanimous:	A group may opt for a unanimous decision or concordance, an undertaking that requires a strong commitment to open and honest dialogue. Although the most difficult to achieve, its results can be very powerful and positive. Although most leaders believe unanimous decision making is too difficult and takes too much time, groups and teams that engage at this level usually have a higher level of trust and openness. This results in faster and more engaged decision making because no games are played. It also results in the highest level of agreement and individual commitment to the outcome.

It is important to be aware of your own preferences for engaging in a group decision-making process. What can often get in the way is not what the group is deciding, or what its decision may be, yet the misalignment of how it is being made.

Key #5: Conflict Management

Of all the ways that we learn about the culture of a group or company, the one that often provides the first and most memorable lesson is when we experience conflict, that is, either when we see others engaged in conflict or we find ourselves engaged in it. Power and influence, rank, position, and role can all be observed in how people tussle with one another. A culture's values are often tested in times of conflict, which reveal how winning and losing is perceived and what values are most important.

A telling aspect of culture can be detected in how participants build coalitions. In some cultures, winning the argument is achieved through the size and strength of the coalition. For most people in a conflict, one of the first steps they take is to look for support. A conflict is usually an expression of anger that results from not getting what one wants or needs. This is natural. Cultures are made up of individuals busy engaging one another to meet their needs. When those needs are not met, people engage in conflict with those they hold responsible. If we observe conflicts in the context of culture, we'll probably be able to identify the source— and chances are it will align to the core values and beliefs of the culture. There are three causes of conflict, and they align to the three sources of human motivation. What is often at the heart of a conflict is that something is perceived to be missing. What people expect most of their culture is quite telling. It could be the need for inclusion and involvement, for recognition of one's performance and capability, or the desire to openly express what one thinks or feels.

Key #6: Incentives and Rewards

Incentives and rewards are intended to reinforce behavior that results in the accomplishment of goals and objectives. The popular approach is to align the incentive, reward, or celebration to the stated measurable goal. The belief is that the more aligned the goal and rewards are, the more likely a person will be to pursue and achieve it. *In the simplest terms, what is measured and rewarded gets done.* The most popular reward is money. This doesn't necessarily mean it is the most effective or the most important to everyone; there is more to human motivation than money. It's just a matter of individual preference and need.

Over the past several decades, surveys and studies on what employees want and what motivates them have focused on the connection of motivation and reward to employee morale, satisfaction, and performance. The list has remained fairly consistent over time, and money usually does not take the top spot, although most people work for money. If money is a given (at whatever level), then what other important influences affect how people feel about their work, their employers, and themselves.

Surveys and studies repeatedly show that wages rank number five or lower as a motivator. The top four to five usually include being appreciated, interesting work and the opportunity for growth, job security, help with personal problems, a collegial work environment, good mangers and coworkers, and feeling part of things.

With the possible exception of job security, the other motivators are all elements of culture. The key to how employees feel is the environment and direct relationship to fellow employees and leaders. This is clear evidence that the need to align how people are incented and rewarded with the right cultural fit is the most powerful lever influencing performance.

When it comes to leading the culture, it's important to recognize the substantial value placed on the employee's direct relationship to managers and leaders. As a company grows, it becomes more challenging to manage and lead people consistently. This fact reinforces the importance of leadership development. For smaller businesses, key leaders are more visible and accessible. The ease with which people can observe, be influenced by, and interpret the leader's behavior requires a consciousness of how easily the culture can be influenced. However small or large the business, how people feel about their managers and leaders is a key source of personal motivation.

Additional considerations that are important to the alignment of incentives and rewards to a company's culture include whether the reward is focused on group or individual performance. Often, combining the two creates tension and raises the question of which is more important. That priority conveys a value that reveals what behavior is more likely to be rewarded and affects the nature of teamwork. A group reward conveys the value that a person's contribution to the group is more important than individual achievement, while a reward focused on the individual conveys the opposite.

Ideally, the two should come together. Individual performance contributes to the group's success, and both are rewarded. However, the two are often interpreted as separate considerations. As a result, people are uncertain of the company's priorities and which behavior will earn them the highest reward. Similarly, when a group's overall success is questioned, members are left wondering at what point it is more beneficial to pursue their individual performance and reward. Such nuances are important. Rather than convey consistent messages as to what is important to the culture, they can create confusion.

Aligning incentives, rewards, and celebration contributes to the emotional aspects of performance. It is important to pay attention to the non-monetary aspects of rewards, including the intrinsic benefits associated with contributing to the mission or vision, the interest in the idealistic nature of the company's brand intention, and relationship with peers who share your personal values and intention. For some, it is the sense of accomplishment and status associated with expertise and the personal recognition one gains. For others, it is the social celebration and the feeling and shared euphoria derived from being a member of a community or high-performing team. As with the other culture keys, the important aspect is the alignment to the values and beliefs of the culture and the expectations of how people interact with and work with one another.

Key #7: Hiring

Extraordinary cultures learn to be really good at hiring the right people. As a culture strengthens and clarifies its alignment to its brand intention, it attracts individuals who are more likely to be good fits. There are two good reasons for this. The first is the emotional connection and affinity on a conscious or subconscious level that people feel for the brand intention and the desire to be involved and connected with it. This is one of the reasons why psychological typing has become a popular component of the hiring process. Not only is it applied to evaluating the alignment of an individual to a specific job function or role, it is also used as a tool for evaluating whether a candidate is a good culture fit.

The second reason is that members of an aligned culture are more apt to share their experience with others, attracting like-minded people seeking employment and new opportunity. This is a valuable asset. Some of the best recruiting is accomplished by the employees of companies who are true believers and invest themselves in brining like-minded and talented people to the company.

To this, add the power of the culture itself. The first two are products of a company's culture. However, in today's world of transparency and information availability, communicating and deliberately marketing your company's culture is an important aspect of attracting the best fitting talent.

Another aspect of alignment, which speaks to how the decision gets made and with what degree of consideration, is to hire deliberately, whether slow or fast. This requires a very clear idea of what competencies, skills, knowledge, and expertise are required for the new employee to succeed. Any new hire should sense that they will be able to perform and meet immediate and longer term performance expectations. A great hire is someone who can meet the criteria of competency and knowledge *and* be a good fit for the culture.

Two other important aspects of the hiring process require alignment. The first concerns the interview process itself. Those involved must be aligned on the scheduling and sequence, aware of the criteria on which a decision will be made and consistent about how candidates are interviewed. It should be clear who is doing the interviewing, what key findings each interviewer is responsible for attaining and reporting, what each interviewers role and areas of inquiry are, and what questions each is responsible for asking. Each person must commit the time necessary to conduct a thoughtful and thorough interview. Taking the time to hire well usually pays long-term dividends. Not hiring well can be very costly.

The second consideration is alignment on how the hiring decision will be made. If this part of the process is unclear, the desired outcome to hire the best candidate can be undermined. One CEO of a sizable company insisted that she delegated the hiring of new employees to the managers and executives and would support their decisions, yet she still wanted to meet each candidate personally. On more than one occasion, the managers and executives involved agreed on a hire only to have the CEO raise doubts, often without much justification. Those involved interpreted her questions as a rejection of the person and moved on to the next candidate.

If a team is making the hiring decision, many of the same principles apply. The team should align on the criteria for the position and role, the information being shared with the interviewee, and what questions are being asked and by whom. Team members may also also be aligned on how the decision will be made, a process that should be made transparent to the candidate. An early display of authenticity and trust invites the candidate to reciprocate and answer questions candidly and forthrightly.

In any interviewing process, it's important to provide the candidate with information. It's much more important to ask questions and listen. It's only through intentional listening that we can determine whether someone has the qualifications for a position and is a good fit for the culture.

The next part of the hiring process occurs after the candidate officially becomes an employee of the company. If the selection process went well, then the individual will already have a pretty good idea of the key elements of the culture, although what the person learned during the hiring process does not provide, by any means, a complete picture. Whether meeting with a leader or a team members or participating in a more complete orientation process, the first days of a new hire's tenure offer the best opportunity for education and assimilation to the company culture.

A good rule of thumb is to share everything about the culture that you have learned since your first day, such as what you would have found helpful on your first day. This includes, aspects of the culture that make it great as well as the challenges and issues it faces. Let new hires know what is expected when conflict happens, how power and influence are used, what to do when things aren't working, and how to find joy and celebrate the work they are engaged in. Let them know how to be successful and contribute to the success of others. When the time comes to teach someone about your company's culture, don't hold back. This aspect of the hiring process is often a lost opportunity, and the new hire is left to finding out about the culture by trial and error. You can't cover every detail or nuance about your culture, yet a little is better than nothing. And more is even better.

Key #8: Role Definition

A company founder and CEO recently eliminated the use of job titles in her professional services company because she never liked the competition for titles and thought the process was outdated and too often took precedence over the level of contribution being made. In fact, with few exceptions, the performance of recently promoted members of her firm declined once they achieved a higher title. She also didn't like how those with more important titles interacted with employees of lesser status. It was an impediment to open and effective communication, hindered the exchange of ideas and the flow of information, and presented a barrier to collaboration. She felt titles created a wall that had to come down.

Making the decision work wasn't easy. Many longer term employees were angered over the loss of the status and recognition they believed that they deservedly earned. Some felt that it would keep the company from attracting talent; they believed that better and more qualified people put a great deal of value in a title and the status that goes with it and that younger people coming into the company looking to build their careers would want a title to add to their résumés.

The CEO, who was interested in performance, noticed that younger upstart employees and those in the middle were performing at higher levels than their superiors, yet she was concerned about the possibility of losing a few of the longer term producers.

She hit on the concept of role definitions, which she felt was more accurate and less constraining than titles. Such definitions allowed people to expand what they were doing and be more creative. Along with broader role definitions, she instituted a more vigorous and evenly distributed pay-for-performance approach. Based on the initial results, she expected the subsequent higher levels of performance would more than offset the risk. Her ultimate goal was to create a better culture.

Role definitions and how they align to culture hold several sources of emotional content. For one thing, as the story demonstrates, role definitions are often tied to titles and offer a response to the human motivation to be competent and have the predictability and status associated with control. Often, a role definition verifies one's place in the hierarchy.

People are interested in putting their talent, knowledge, and expertise to use and having an opportunity to further develop. In focusing on how roles are defined, one important factor is how people are expected to apply their competencies to their work. Another is how role definition can be used to engage people to learn, grow, and expand their capabilities. Rather than focusing only on the present and what needs to happen from day to day, connecting the current definition to the future provides an awareness of how a role can evolve and what expertise, skills, and knowledge will be required to get there. It offers a remarkably powerful way to align an individual's development with the company's future vision.

When a person is given a defined role, it confirms their presence and verifies their significance. It provides a sense of belonging and inclusion in a group or team. With a role comes a function, and one can rely on that function to contribute to the whole. The sense of interdependence can become a source of motivation to contribute and be of service to one another. This can help establish a consciousness of the reciprocity of communication and the sharing of information and ideas. Given the need for group members to communicate with one another, conveying this aspect of team performance through role definition can benefit the individual as well as others members of the group.

Finally, role definition often provides evidence of who someone is or confirms who a person aspires to be. Often such validation signifies proof of an individual's association with a cause or ideal. Often, the role doesn't need to impart status. Rather, it demonstrates that it is an extension of one's personality.

Role definitions also convey expectations about how jobs are performed, how tasks are carried out, and what is required of team members. The definition of a role can be specific to a particular area of expertise or it can be broad and apply to multiple facets of work and function.

Role definitions can include other pieces of information about how jobs and tasks are accomplished, including involvement in problem solving, decision making, and individual empowerment. Clarity of roles and the expectations associated with them help to provide a framework for individuals to interpret how they fit into how the company and how the company successfully creates and delivers its products or services to the customer.

Key #9: Customer Interface

How a culture interfaces with the customer has changed dramatically over time. Along with advances in how we market and sell, the leveraging of technology and the media, and the innovations that have propelled convenience and availability, companies have a broader set of powerful choices for connecting with the customer. At the same time, some things haven't changed that much. One constant over time is that every employee can influence customers. An assembly line worker at a car company a hundred years ago promoted his company's brand when talking about his work to others. He was interfacing with customers and influencing them.

At some point, every employee interfaces with the customer, often without realizing it. When it comes to the culture key of customer interface, *how people feel about the culture of the company they are a part of will directly or indirectly influence its customers.* With this broader view of everyone's informal involvement in a company's relationship with its customers, let's turn to how companies and cultures more formally organize their interfaces with the customer, including how a company arranges and systematizes its functions and teams to execute its vision and strategies.

Two important aspects of alignment need to be considered. The first is the culture and how the organization of customer interface aligns to it. The second is how well it aligns to the brand intention, including how the product or service is delivered to the customer and what that experience is intended to look and feel like. Depending on the product or service, the company may place responsibility for customer interface with a few select individuals who perform that function on behalf of the whole.

It may serve a company well to take a team-based approach through which several employees work together to interface with the customer. If the intention is to develop consistent ongoing relationships with customers, team structure can work very well. Over time, it allows the customer to interface with the same group of people and enjoy a set of predictable relationships.

Another form of teaming, aimed at offering multiple forms of expertise and competency in service to the customer, is an approach similar to that taken in project management. While it may appear unplanned, it allows the customer to interact and have access to those with specific expertise, proficiency, or knowledge. This aligns well when the product or service being delivered conveys a high level of technical or subject knowledge. By directly delivering a high level of specific competency, the customer is influenced to have an increased level of trust.

Companies can also adopt a more fluid design, an informal approach through which any company member interested in working with or more intentionally selling to the customer has the opportunity to do so. Often, this allows those who have a natural desire to interface with customers to do so, even if they have other role responsibilities. Employees are given the choice and can empower themselves in a manner that is mutually beneficial. For people who have been in jobs with limited or no interaction with customers, working in a culture and structure that conveys such empowerment offers the opportunity to explore new opportunities and develop customer service skills.

Companies exist to sell and deliver a product or service to its customers. When a company's customer interface is misaligned, the customer experiences it. Unfortunately, this happens all too often. A mistake made in organizing customer interface is to overly focus on the internal workings and processes of a company, leaving out the most important part of the equation—satisfying the customer.

Key #10: Teamwork

There are a great many definitions and approaches to teamwork. Most companies include teamwork as one of their values and beliefs. If it's not listed as a core value or belief, it will show up in how the company describes itself. Its importance is obvious. Bring together two or more people with a common goal and you have the basic ingredients of a team. From there, it's just a matter of scaling it. Without teamwork, things don't get done.

Teamwork is natural to human beings, yet success requires a great deal of effort because the quality of the outcome is a reflection of the quality of the team's members. It's easy to bring people together; the challenge is the teambuilding that follows. To create an aligned and high-performing team requires dedication and commitment to developing successful relationships among the members.

A high-performing team is an aligned group of individuals committed to creating extraordinary results for themselves and one another.

The fundamental characteristics of high-performing teams that support the alignment of its members are:

- A focus on results
- A strong team culture
- Aligned leadership
- Open communication

- High-performing members
- Assessment and improvement

Most other aspects of teamwork, including trust, mutual respect, constructive conflict management, and decision making, fit into these six characteristics.

One specific definition of high performance does not fit all teams. A team that works best aligns the ideal team member to the other characteristics of the team, its values, and its goals. This means that the right fit can only be defined when one knows what the team's culture team is or is intended to be. This includes how an individual is expected to communicate, assume responsibility for results, and work with fellow team members. Every team has a definition of what it means for members to get along with one another.

The definition of a high-performing team member stems from its uniqueness. While some of the characteristics of teamwork remain consistent, every team is unique in, among other ways, how power and influence, reward, decision making, problem solving, and conflicts are managed. When multiple teams function similarly, there tends to be greater alignment than when they operate differently. Being able to distinguish the likenesses and differences is often required when teams work with one another. The larger a company, the more complex the team-to-team relationships may be. This is why using teamwork as a key to alignment is so valuable.

Three primary approaches provide an initial framework. The first is organizing a team based on expertise, competencies, and areas of specialization. Larger companies accomplish this using approaches adapted from project management, which allow more flexible frameworks for teaming and moving people from project team to project team to take advantage of their expertise and specific competencies.

Another way to see this is through a matrix structure. A focus on leveraging specific competencies and expertise areas can also result in teams that are centered on a certain content area or are organized to perform a particular function, such as a team of designers in a product development function or an in-house sales team where each individual is responsible for his or her own performance. The key characteristic that creates individual-to-team alignment is the demonstration of expertise, competency, and knowledge.

Another primary approach is cross-functional teams. In these teams, role definitions generally require that members be generalists rather than specialists. For example, in a human resources team, members might move in and out of various roles and jobs, including payroll, benefits administration, recruitment, training, orientation, and employment law compliance, even though each requires a certain level of expertise and knowledge. In smaller companies, the generalist or small group of generalists cross-functionally meet the overall performance expectations of the team, often filling in for or helping one another. Characteristics that are looked for and align an individual to the team are a willingness to collaborate and build consensus, placing a priority on contributing to the performance of the team, and an ability to move in and out of the various roles within the team.

The third primary form of teaming focuses on individual freedom and the alignment of each person's contribution to the central cause or ideals of the team. Often in a hybrid fashion, team members have a great deal of autonomy and can take both generalist and expertise-oriented roles. What differs is the motivation of the group and how it is brought to life through the team members. The key characteristic of alignment is whether they demonstrate a commitment to the idealistic values and goals of the whole.

These three approaches create a point of reference and a framework through which you can identify the traits and characteristics of team formation and alignment. Remember that every team is unique; the more aligned a team is to its desired goals and outcomes and the more it is focused on results, the better it performs. The more open and informal the communication, the better its ability to confront and effectively deal with conflicts and disagreements among its members. And, the more openly members of team communicate, the better their ability to assess how the team performs and how to improve.

Two other aspects of teamwork are worth mentioning. The first concerns external relationships. The better the members align and work with one another, the better they typically work with other teams, groups, and customers. Sometimes other teams and people in a company are a team's internal customers. Whomever the team is interacting with, maintaining productive and healthy external relationships is important to success; resources, communication, information sharing, and collaborative relationships depend on it.

A second aspect is related to leadership alignment. Leadership has a high degree of influence on the culture of a team and how well it is aligned. High-performing teams generally have leaders who are aligned to how the team plans, makes decisions, solves problems, and carries out the other aspects of teaming and performance. Leaders also influence how team members align their behaviors to the values and beliefs of the team and a company, which is critical. Too often leaders are misaligned to the teams they lead. As we'll explore in Chapter Ten, aligned leadership is essential to overall alignment and a vital factor to success.

Key #11: Structure

When it comes to the structural alignment of a company, structure follows form.

Frequently, leaders and their companies fall into the trap of over-relying on experiences, models, and frameworks in building and running companies. One of the most alluring pitfalls is organizational and team structure. Maybe because it has been done so many times or because we have organizational charts burned indelibly into our brains, our ideas about how to organize and structure companies into functional components is given the least amount of creativity and forethought. Many leaders design and structure their companies in two interesting ways. One is from the inside out. While this allows them to focus on the operational elements of how they create and deliver a product or service, it often fails to put the most important aspect of the business—the customer—out in front. As a result, the organization's structure ends up misaligned to the customer experience, and the company may struggle for a long time to overcome this. Even if the company succeeds, it may still not be working as well as it could. The evidence of misalignment are the problems and conflicts that are constantly at play between the various parts and teams within a company, its individual members, and its customers.

The second is adopting the design and structure that works for another company, and which is unlikely to fully align with and serve yours. The structure of a company like Whole Foods differs from Wal-Mart's for good reason. They have different brand intentions and customer expectations and interactions differ. Their supply-chain systems differ and require distinct approaches to organizing and aligning their workforces. They also differ in how teaming takes place. Wal-Mart separates employees into functional units and groups, each with its own goals and responsibility resting with the leader. Whole Foods is structured around teams. Each store has an average of ten self-managed teams with a designated leader. The leaders and team members share group responsibility for leading the store. Wal-Mart has its own organizational structure, forms of teaming, cultures, and brand intentions. Customers buy from the company for different reasons. While both companies are very different from one another, they are both very well aligned.

The successful design and implementation of an aligned structure requires focusing on three key aspects: (1) how the company interfaces with the customer; (2) how the work of creating and delivering the product or service in alignment to the brand intention is done; and, (3) how its members team with one another. The structure of a company serves best when it is aligned to the culture. When the culture is forced to work within a misaligned structure, people seldom perform to their full potential. An aligned company or team structure is a vital ingredient to a healthy company.

Key #12: Aligned Values

The last of the twelve alignment keys is certainly not the least important. All twelve are important. When necessary, each takes on a role of greater significance in the alignment of your company's culture. However, the alignment of values is often not given enough attention. This, despite the fact that in many instances, leaders and managers are not given more than of values and beliefs through which to define their cultures.

When it comes to leading culture, aligning values is essential. It's simply not good enough to hang the words on the wall, post them on your website, or repeat them at company meetings. For people to understand and take responsibility for them, leaders must talk about them constantly and consistently. They must explain what the values mean, what they represent, and how significant they are to the company's culture. Leaders must role model and relentlessly reinforce them. The core values of a culture cannot be overstated, overcommunicated, or overly reinforced. They are that important. Values define the core of a culture and describe the intended human experience.

What follows are three commonly used words that are frequently employed as company values, along with three distinct interpretations of them which. While some commonalities exist, they also provide significantly different intellectual and emotional responses. Once you've read through these examples, look at the words used to describe your company's culture and perform the same exercise. The goal is to clearly articulate for your culture the meaning of the words that are your core values.

Empowerment. Definitions of empowerment are as wide ranging as its meaning within the context of culture. Empowerment often means that someone is given permission to act. For example, a construction company is working to improve its safety record and wants supervisors to take greater responsibility on job sites. In the past, supervisors feared criticism or negative feedback for slowing down progress and were afraid of being thought inefficient or less cost effective. As a result, they hesitated to stop workers to make changes or to commit the time and resources required to do things differently. After a series of worker injuries, the company's leadership told supervisors they could, if necessary, stop the work that was being performed and make changes that would increase worker safety. They were also told that, prior to taking action, they should first check with their respective managers. Workers who identified risks were also empowered to take their concerns to the supervisor. *In this culture, empowerment is synonymous with permission granting.*

Another example involves an onsite software development firm where small groups, led by a team leader, worked directly with the customer. At times, the teams hired extra help to meet deadlines or respond to specific requirements because the CEO believes that customer service and meeting project timelines is critical to success. He repeatedly communicates the view that team leaders, as well as onsite team members, are empowered to do what it takes to please the customer without asking for permission, including hiring to get the project done on time and meet the project requirements. *In this scenario, the definition of empowerment is the authority to make decisions.*

The president of a hospitality company tells stories of empowerment to employees at its properties. She continuously stresses the idea that anyone in the company, regardless of their role, can take action or be of extraordinary service to leave a lasting impression on a guest. One evening, a mother arrived at a location with two children. The father had stayed behind to deal with a medical emergency and promised to join the family at the hotel en route to the hotel, his car broke down, and he was stranded in a small town over two hours away from the hotel, where he needed to wait until morning to have his car repaired. When learning of the family's dilemma, a front desk clerk decided to make the more than four-hour drive to pick up the father and bring him to the hotel that night. He also connected his guest with a local mechanic to have the car towed and repaired. *In this culture, the definition of empowerment is to be inspired to be extraordinary.*

Respect. In alignment to culture, the word can give attention to one's competency, one's rank or authority, the behaviors associated with mutual respect, or reciprocity. The three scenarios start with the same set of characters and the same challenge.

The setting is a conference room in the main building of a healthcare company. The company's four core values of Respect, Teamwork, Excellence, and Quality Care are prominently displayed throughout the facility. The CEO is meeting with his executive staff to talk about his decision to hire a new chief medical officer. The CEOs choice for the position, an outside candidate, is not the group's preferred choice. The members prefer an internal candidate whom they believe, based on over six years with the company, is a better match. The CEO thinks the outside candidate is a better choice because he has already held a similar position.

In the first scenario, the CEO shares his decision with the members of the executive team. When asked for their thoughts, a few share their opinions. The CEO voices his disagreement and soon the team members are arguing. The CEO is unwavering in his decision. Eventually, the CEO and the group turn to one executive and ask for her input. In the past, she has been a good source of insight and has held similar positions to the one being filled. When asked for her expert opinion, she shares a number of factors with the team and recommends the company hire the internal candidate. The CEO respects her expertise and has confidence in her choice. He realigns his position, and the hospital hires the internal candidate. *In this culture, the meaning of respect conveys deference to one's expertise, competency, experience, and proven capability.*

In the second scenario, the CEO starts the meeting by sharing his thoughts and explaining that he is leaning toward hiring the external candidate. He then invites the members of the executive team to share their opinions. The group, including the CEO, is soon engaged in a dialogue. They ask questions of one another, ask for more information and thoughts, and make sure that everyone's perspective is heard and understood. In the end, the team, including the CEO, make a shared decision to hire the internal candidate. *In this culture, the meaning of respect is assuring that everyone is engaged with one another and heard.*

In the third scenario, the CEO shares his decision with the team and asks if anyone has a different opinion. In the days leading up to this meeting, several members of the executive team have discussed their preference for the internal candidate. When asked for their opinions in the meeting, a couple of the executives briefly share their thoughts and opinions. Showing respect for his role and position, they look to the CEO to make his decision. He tells them that, acting in the best interest of the hospital, he has decided to stick with his decision to hire the external candidate. *In this scenario, the meaning of respect is deference to position, title, or rank, and the authority that accompanies it.*

Trust. This often-used term has multiple meanings and applications, particularly because of its significance to customer relations. For example, a team member asks a fellow member to contribute to completing a project on time. He agrees, and she stresses the importance of his contribution by telling him that she trusts he'll get it done. *In this culture, trust means being able to rely on another person and be confident they will follow through.*

In another scenario, a manager asks an employee to take on a very demanding set of tasks that have a high degree of risk associated with them. They require a high level of decision-making capability. He has chosen to delegate them to her because of her strong competencies. While committing to the challenge, she expresses her concern about the complex nature of the work. He tells her that he trusts she can do it. *In this culture, the meaning of trust is having confidence in someone's ability, competency, and know-how.*

In the next example, a team is quickly coming up on a deadline, and several of the members are concerned about whether or not the team can come together to meet its goals. There have been several conflicts along the way, raising doubt about how committed everyone is to meeting their responsibilities. To be successful, each team member must deliver his or her individual contribution. As the deadline nears, one team members pulls the team together by sharing his belief that if they focus on emotionally supporting one another, the deadline will be met. *In this culture, the meaning of trust is having faith and believing in the possibilities.*

Finally, an employee approaches his manager for feedback. He was recently given a new and challenging assignment, was second-guessing his capabilities, and had doubts about how well he was doing. He not only agreed to the new assignment as an opportunity for career advancement opportunity; he also accepted it to advance financially and improve his family's living conditions. If he finds that he is not meeting the expectations of his manager, he can take action to avoid the negative consequences of failing. He asks her to be honest, telling her that he trusts that she will be truthful with him. *In this culture, the trust is people being honest with one another.*

As you can see, the words we use to define values and beliefs come to life through human behavior and interaction. Earlier in this chapter, as part of the definition of culture, I indicated that culture could be defined as how people treat one another. Much like promises, a culture's values and beliefs offer a consistent perspective and shared sense of how people in a company or team treat each other and how they treat the customer. As with any promise or expectation, it's very important to bring values into the spoken realm and to explore what they mean. This is an ongoing obligation of leaders and a requirement of those they lead.

TUNING THE CULTURE KEYS

The twelve culture keys are not the only ingredients that define a company's culture. If you look closely, you may find that there are traits specific to your culture that can be keys for alignment. The twelve keys are a framework—a common set of characteristics—you can use to observe and measure your culture and the culture of any company or team offer a great start in the right direction.

THE 12 CULTURE KEYS

Power and Influence
Planning and Goal Setting
Problem Solving
Decision Making
Conflict Management
Incentive and Reward
Hiring
Role Definition
Customer Interface
Teamwork
Structure
Aligned Values

NINE

Aligning Culture

*Alignment provides predictability. Predictability provides safety.
Safety provides confidence. Confidence provides performance.*

I'll never forget, when at the age of nine, my father took me to New York's
Yankee Stadium to see my first baseball game. As we walked through the
tunnel into the bright light afternoon sun, I was instantly mesmerized by
the vastness of the stands, the brilliance of the green lawn across the field,
the famous white veneer from which Yankee banners hung, and the
proudly displayed flags, representing the team's World Championships.

This is a place of heroes. I could feel the energy that electrified the
stadium an hour before the game even started. I was drawn into and ab-
sorbed by Yankee culture. When the players burst onto the field in the
famous Yankee pinstripes with the swagger of winners, cheering fans rose
to their feet, and I experienced an emotion I will never forget.

As a management and leadership consultant, I pay a great deal of attention to what I observe, how I feel, and what I infer when first walking
into a building or room. I am especially sensitive to the environment and
the energy of the employees and how they interact with one another. I
listen intently to how they speak to one another. No matter the venue, a
dynamic is always present that consciously or unconsciously contributes
to how we feel about our experience. It is always the human quality that
affects us.

This happened when I first walked through the processing and packing plant of Blue Diamond Almonds, a growers-owned cooperative of

over 3,000 California almond farmers. From the moment I interacted with the woman in the security booth and stepped onto the company's grounds, I experienced a sense of casualness, calm, wellbeing, and ease, even though a great deal of activity was going on around me. There's an energy that permeates a company's culture and contributes to how everyone—employee or visitor feels.

Over the last four to five decades, Blue Diamond's brand name has become increasingly familiar worldwide. The company distributes millions of pounds of almonds to over 95 countries, and it continues to grow. Globally, almonds are the number one nut, with consumption growing steadily at 10 percent per year. Blue Diamond is the world's largest processor and marketer of almonds, and California accounts for 80 percent of the world's production. Like any great company, Blue Diamond owes it success to its aligned culture. Often we discover that the origin and roots of a culture can be found in the values and beliefs of the founders—in this case, 230 California almond farmers in 1909, which remain its guiding principles. This is certainly true of Blue Diamond. The founders' commitment to partnership, innovation, integrity, and quality remain the guiding forces of its current culture. Today, its 3,000 grower-owners are a diverse group who operate orchards ranging from 10 to thousands of acres. Their goal is for each to personally benefit from their membership and trust in the integrity and commitment of those responsible for leading the company. This common thread is evident in the company's culture and its employees' commitment to the member farmers.

In the 1920s, scientists discovered that almonds were an excellent source of protein and minerals. Almond sales exploded, and Blue Diamond's brand intention of physical wellbeing came into being. During World War II, chocolate bars with almonds were given to troops to improve nutrition. This further elevated almonds' nutritional status, and their popularity grew. The natural foods explosion of recent decades paved the way for Blue Diamond's very successful marketing, which targets the health-conscious market. The trend is expected to continue. By leveraging its brand intention of physical wellbeing with its capability for product innovation worldwide, Blue Diamond has successfully expanded the brand's sphere of influence to include the rapidly growing markets of India, China, and Eastern Europe.

Bruce Lish's relationship to Blue Diamond is representative of it's employee experiences. He began working there 42 years ago as a part-timer while he pursued a career as a professional baseball player. He stayed with the company for the next four decades working in a variety of positions. He readily accepted opportunities and new roles, even when he had minimal knowledge, often cultivating his competencies and skills as the job required them. Bruce personally developed and grew with the company, which is not unusual at Blue Diamond, where personal development and ownership are continuously reinforced. Eventually, he became General Manager of Operations and a member of the executive team.

As with other employees I talked to, Bruce described the company's culture as one of family. It is an organization comprised of long-term employees who develop lasting relationships with one another. They see themselves as members of a big team in which each individual displays a pride of ownership and defines his or her own path to improvement and development. Employees are given the opportunity to pursue personal satisfaction, enrichment, and empowerment. Employees have daily control over workflow, a responsibility that results in an ongoing effort to identify improvements and work in collaboration with team members to track performance and create change. Like Bruce, employees are given the opportunity to learn and develop the competencies and skills needed to take on new roles and responsibilities and to grow through them. That expertise and skill results in the continuous innovation—creating new products and offerings, opening new markets, and collaborating with its partners—and growth the company enjoys.

Blue Diamond Almonds culture preference is authenticity, and it successfully integrates traits of participation and expertise to innovate and deliver quality. The values that guide its leadership and employees are commitment and integrity. The company's culture is powerfully aligned to its vision of delivering the benefits of almonds to the world, which has been at the core of its brand for over a century.

Creating and leading an aligned culture is one of the more demanding tests of leadership. It applies to CEOs, business owners, and anyone in a leadership role. Successful alignment begins with a framework, knowing what the keys of culture are, and knowing how to apply them. This requires a keen awareness about what motivates individual and group behavior and how these forces influence *how* things get done.

ITS ALWAYS ABOUT PEOPLE

Cultures are groups of people. A company can have many moving parts that function to produce a product or service and succeed in winning the customer. There are many choices about what market strategies to pursue or what internal changes are needed to improve performance. The twelve culture keys are all about what motivates people and aligns them to work together. It always comes back to one thing: It's always about people.

The three human motivations: (1) the level of attention we receive; (2) the level of competency we achieve; and (3) the level of acceptance we attain are the keys to understanding the patterns and norms of behavior within a culture, how a culture defines success, and what constitutes acceptable and unacceptable behavior. They are the drivers to how values and beliefs come about and how well people align to them. They allow leaders to strategically use the culture keys to create alignment and a sense of predictability that supports healthy patterns of individual and group behavior.

Cultures result from the interaction of people in groups, from how they influence one another to get their individual and group needs met. We all seek fulfillment and, as a result, all three sources of motivation are present in us individually and in the culture of the groups we form.

As individuals, we have distinct personalities—behavioral characteristics that reflect our psychological make-up and our experiences and result in our uniqueness. Our own mix of traits and qualities guide our personae and the behaviors we use to influence others; they are manifested through the attitudes and dispositions we show to the world.

In working with others and fitting into a culture, the traits we demonstrate, our likes and dislikes, the type of team player we are, how we compete, how willing we are to collaborate, our willingness to engage in conflict, our eagerness to hear what others have to say, our impatience, our insecurities and fears, what makes us happy, what angers us, and what brings us joy and contentment, how we express and communicate our values and beliefs, how we judge what is good and bad, right and wrong, and how we interpret what is moral and immoral all come into play.

Through all of our actions—the choices we make and everything we do and say—we convey the preferences of our personalities and express our wants, needs, and desires. While every person is affected by each source of motivation, everyone shows a preference, to some degree, for one of them. This also applies to how one leads. As we'll explore in Chapter Ten, a leader's personal preference will generally show in his or her leadership style and strategic inclinations.

THE THREE CULTURE PREFERENCES

Cultures are groups of people motivated by their needs. We engage in collective action with others to achieve what we individually want and need and to contribute to a shared outcome. The three human needs are attention, competency, and acceptance. In the context of culture, these are satisfied through the behaviors associated with the level of participation, the use of expertise, and the authenticity with which people communicate with one another. These provide observable and measurable means through which we can assess how a company or team goes about getting things done and how people interact with one another.

In cultures, the need for attention is met through *participation*. This is communicated through engagement in collaborative and inclusive approaches and group processes, the level of social interaction, and how individuals are included in the various processes and actions that are undertaken.

The need for competency is met through *expertise*, which is communicated by how personal achievement is rewarded, how hierarchy relates to competency and rank, and the amount of control and authority granted to individuals based on their skills, knowledge, and competency.

The need for acceptance is met through *authenticity*, which is demonstrated through openness and honesty and the ability of members to freely express what they think, see, and feel.

Just as every person will show a level of preference for one of the three human motivations, the same is true of cultures, where it is the result of how people influence one another and how they work with one another to get things done. Every culture, regardless of size, displays norms and patterns of behavior that reflect its preference; the more clearly defined and predictable that preference is, the more likely the members are to perform at high levels.

This is an important aspect of how one intentionally and successfully leads an aligned culture. By constantly and consistently defining and aligning how things are done, the preferences of a culture provide a sense of safety to its members, tell its members what is acceptable and unacceptable, and explain how to take part in and contribute to success. Aligned cultures offer consistency and predictability to groups in which people feel safe and believe they can act without fear. In turn, this confidence gives people the courage to take risks, which allows them to engage their imaginations and express their creativity. Creativity is the engine of innovation, and aligned cultures are innovative cultures. The people in them love to perform, contribute to the vision and mission of a company, and be a part of its shared success.

Some practical aspects of alignment are worth investigating here.

The first is that *every culture is unique*. It is important to observe and measure those traits and characteristics that make it so and, when they serve the company well, to integrate them into the culture's intentional alignment. Although you may be tempted to believe that absolute alignment of the culture keys is necessary, that is not the case. Aspects and practices that reflect the traits of the other two preferences can be used in service to a company's culture to leverage a unique quality without which the company would not perform the same way.

That said, *the clarity of alignment to one culture preference is an important ingredient of success.* Companies and teams that lack clarity or try to balance all three preferences—participation, expertise, and authenticity— are generally grappling with performance issues. In most cases, the challenges and performance issues are predictable. The lack of clarity, opposing viewpoints, and differing perspectives, as well as the coalitions that develop in support of them, typically result in a lack of cooperation and the failures of poor teamwork. Often, the resulting "us versus them" mentality finds its way to the customer.

A better approach is to identify the qualities typically associated with the other two cultural preferences and strategically use them in service of the preference with which your company is aligned. The key to success is to define and articulate the reasoning behind the strategy and clearly define the intended outcomes and influence. A good way to make such decisions is to ask, "What is in the best interest of the business?" and to clearly and consistently communicate it.

It's relatively easy to create confusion by not being clear. In my experience, companies that measure fairly equally across the three preferences have a host of issues and dysfunctional patterns of behavior and interactions. In most cases, this approach results in the formation of coalitions, each arguing for its own way of doing things. *Much like a multipersonality disorder, it's not a good idea to have a multiculture disorder. It confuses everyone, including your customer.*

When one part of the company has a culture preference that is not aligned with the rest of the company, it is known as a subculture. The two are often at odds. This can lead to many of the same issues as occur when a company's culture preference is ill defined, including the ongoing conflicts the culture clash fuels. Usually, when a subculture exists and causes severe problems, the best solution is to change it, although this is difficult without changing the people. The path to culture change is almost always turnover, which often includes, or begins with, the leader.

Exceptions occur when it is in the best interest of the business to maintain a subculture. There are *three ways to integrate a subculture successfully.* The first is for the leader or team of leaders to *clearly articulate the business reasons and strategy behind having a subculture and to consistently communicate how it is in service to the company as a whole.* The second is that the leaders themselves *have an ongoing conversation to assure that they are all continuously in alignment on their shared strategy.* This is vital. If the leaders are not aligned and do not communicate in an aligned fashion, their respective team members will follow their lead. When the leaders of different teams and groups are in conflict, their team members will be too. From individual workgroups to large business units and divisions, when the leaders are not aligned, the "us against them" attitudes they display influence the people they lead. In some instances, the legacies of leaders who are in ongoing dysfunctional conflict with one another have a long-lasting effect on the companies they led. Companies risk failure, and do fail, because of such misalignment.

The third way is *an ongoing effort by leaders to coach the people they lead*, including sharing the strategy and plan for the subculture, the goals and outcomes the integration is to achieve, how the approaches to work and how getting things done may differ, and how to integrate the differences to create successful working relationships among the groups. There are times when leaders of companies collaborate and work together as a team, yet the groups for which they are responsible do not. Typically, the cause is that the leaders are not spending enough time communicating and coaching their team members on how to achieve success. When it comes to successfully integrating a subculture into the broader, larger culture, leaders cannot overcommunicate or coach enough.

The knowledge and skills required to effectively manage conflict and disagreements must always be a part of coaching. As differing cultures will have their own approaches and norms for managing conflict, a focus on coaching people about the nuances and approaches to creating success between cultures is vital. When it comes to coaching employees about the integration and alignment of culture, communication is often the skill leaders should focus on. This is often true of any coaching relationship.

Before problems arise, leaders should always start to develop the skills necessary to coach others and to assure that others receive the same knowledge and skills. All too often, we wait for trial and error to do its work. That's not good leadership.

THROWING SPAGHETTI

A great deal of power comes with knowing how a culture works and understanding its unique characteristics. One way this power is manifested is predictability. Sometimes strategies that initially look good are, right from the outset, headed for failure; great ideas, in a relatively short time, become bad ones; and, despite good intentions, a change results in more grief, conflict, and disruption than value.

Today, we all have access to a large quantity of information that encourages us to be innovative and continuously make the changes that result in higher levels of performance and success. Ideas flow like water and can be as intoxicating as a fine wine. We are exposed to a multitude of management and leadership thinking through books, blogs, videos, and other media. Still, it's difficult to know what will work and what won't. Some ideas immediately look great and inviting—after all, another company built its success on them. As a result we set out to implement the concept only to eventually conclude that it doesn't work. It's like throwing dry spaghetti against the wall and expecting it to stick.

In my experience, the most frequent cause of failure in implementing a new strategy or change is its misalignment to the culture. It doesn't fit. For example, one company with a hierarchal structure and a top-down leadership approach decided to engage its people in increased collaboration after several of the company's leaders attended a conference on self-directed teams. They thought if they could get everyone working in self-directed teams, it would force employees to communicate more and help break down the company's functional silos.

They began implementing the change by putting frontline employees into self-directed work teams and assigning middle managers to cross-functional leadership teams. Over the course of eight months, the company sent line staff through team training aimed at developing the collaboration and problem-solving skills required. They also sent managers to a two-day workshop on team leadership skills. A year later, they realized that despite reorganizing employees into designated teams and their investment in training, the behavior of leaders and employees had not changed. Decisions were still top down and midlevel leaders were not collaborating any more than before with one another or their employees.

Just because you realign relationships and workgroups doesn't mean that the behaviors of those involved will change. We can question whether two days of training will convince managers to act differently, yet the real reason the strategy failed was that it did not fit the culture. Self-directed and cross-functional teaming are great ideas. Although they work well in some companies, they will not work in every culture. The source of an idea is also important. When you come across an idea, theory, or approach to how to best run, lead, or work in a company, it is important to recognize the preferences of the person or people providing it. Whether it is a writer, consultant, coach or other provider, each has preferences and sets of experiences that shape their view of the world and how it works. Those preferences will show themselves in the approaches they advocate. That doesn't make them right or wrong. They just don't fit.

Not every idea or approach will contribute to the alignment of your company. Just because the Toyota Way works in some companies doesn't mean it will work in others. While Six Sigma works well in some cultures, it may be doomed from the start in another (think Starbucks). Too often, when the approach doesn't fit the culture not only will the initiative or strategy fail, it can result in disruption, negatively impact the performance, misalign a culture, and damage the trust in leadership. It can also have a significant negative influence on the customer. Furthermore, it often takes a long time to recover.

When an idea, strategy, or an approach to teaming aligns with a culture, it will generally succeed. When it doesn't, it fails. Replicating or chasing someone else's idea of a best practice will not always bring success. It's much more about having a healthy, aligned company.

It always comes back to asking the key questions. Is the strategy in alignment with or will it further the company's alignment? Does the strategy and its implementation align to your culture? Will the practice or strategy support and further align the company's performance? Will it make us better as a company?

REMEMBER WHO YOU ARE

I'd like to again emphasize *that every culture is unique.* Therefore, each company has to contend with its own alignments and misalignments.

What is right and wrong comes back to what works and doesn't work for each individual company or team. The three culture preferences are a means through which to assess, strategize, and take the actions that best serves your company's or team's culture and result in the highest level of success.

Lastly, I encourage you to *always be connected to your own individual preferences*; they provide a clarifying lens through which you'll be able to find your personal alignments and misalignments, better understand why you enjoy working in one situation over another, and gain insights into your personal leadership preferences. Understanding the three preferences allows you to see how they connect to your values and beliefs.

THE PARTICIPATION PREFERENCE

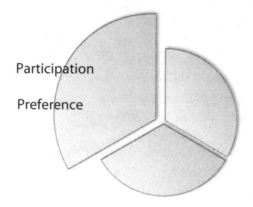

A small, highly specialized company that builds intricate prototype machinery and instruments illustrates a participation culture. Its typical customers include the designers and makers of medical devices, diagnostics instruments, fluid control devices, and other complicated and specialty designed machinery. Often, the company manufactures small batches of very particular, highly technical tools. During its twenty–year history, the company's founder and president, John, built deeply trusted relationships with his clients and carved a strong niche in its regional market. Early on, as the result of these relationships, John was introduced to several larger multinational companies with regional operations, which resulted in ongoing relationships from which the company continues to benefit.

The company's employees are treated as family, and turnover is rare. When he first started the company, John implemented a profit-sharing system that is still in use. Several longer term employees have small percentages of ownership. John includes the part owners as well as other team leaders in most decisions. When one of teams does an exemplary job, the entire company celebrates. The company holds quarterly meetings and twice a year, for the holiday season and in the summer, employees and their families come together for a special event.

Employees are organized into teams, many of which have had the same membership for years. The teams are cross-functional and have direct relationships with customers. Every morning, at 8:10, all employees gather in the lunchroom for the company-wide morning update. John doesn't do much except show up; the teams discuss their projects, how they're coming along, and what new projects are on the horizon. Because the teams share equipment and workspaces, the coordination process the employees engage in is important in successfully meeting timelines. With a focus on customer deliverables, decisions regarding resource allocation and scheduling are made collaboratively and are usually taken care of at the morning update. Members of the accounting team, purchasing, logistics, and human resources are all present at the meeting. The time spent together every morning allows members of teams, when needed, to step in to help another team.

Performance is very stringently measured at the company; team and individual quality and accuracy are constantly scrutinized. Team members take a great deal of pride in assuring that everyone's role is well executed. Employees are trained across all the technical areas, and team members are responsible for mentoring and teaching one another. An ongoing reporting takes place at the morning update. If an issue arises, the expectation is that people will come together to solve the problem quickly and effectively. John likes to point out that working at the company isn't for everyone because of the high demands team members put on each other's performance and the level of responsibility every employee has to keep commitments to fellow team members. The one reason John has had to fire employees was their failure to keep their promises, thereby letting down their fellow team members. With rare exception, these firings were supported by the team the employee was a member of.

Often, when customers come to visit, the entire team spends social time, including dinner, with them. There is a small recreational area with picnic tables, a barbeque pit, a volleyball court, and a bocce court dedicated to connecting employees with one another. When the weather is good, most employees enjoy lunches together and engage each other socially.

Regardless of what a company does and what industry it competes in, it will have culture traits that we're familiar with because they are common to many companies. At the same time, these traits make every company's culture unique and define its cultural preference.

John's company is a good example of a culture with a participation preference. Such cultures often refer to themselves as family-like and pride themselves on inclusivity. Motivation comes from a high level of involvement. People expect to be receive attention and be heard, which results in mutual respect.

Using the twelve culture keys, the following is a typical profile of a participation culture.

Power and Influence is gained through participation and involvement. Those most aligned with the culture are typically seen as amiable, friendly, and outgoing, and a great deal of influence comes from these traits, as well as good listening skills. Someone who collaborates well with others will align well to this preference.

Planning and goal setting is accomplished through involvement and sharing. Large group processes that involve everyone are most likely to result in success. Methods for planning and effectively managing change include brainstorming, shared planning approaches, and processes that broadly include and engage employees. The concept of selecting individual change champions is misaligned, and those who desire to separate from the team are generally not going to succeed. In a participation culture, people who are asked to be change champions will go to the group and collaborate and build team consensus. Measurement of performance against goals is shared openly and inclusively.

Problem solving is a shared and team-work driven process that offers the opportunity for engagement, participation, and involvement. When someone has an issue that needs to be resolved or a challenge to be confronted, it is best served by getting the team together. When a mistake is made, in most cases the team will fix it together. When dealing with a challenge that threatens one of its members, "we're all in this together" is a common response. It gives them an opportunity to engage socially, participate in the process, and make a contribution.

In a participation culture, *decision making* is also a shared and group-driven process. In John's company, a high degree of involvement and information sharing is required; commitment to a decision is lessened when people feel uninformed or left out of the loop. Often, leaders in participation cultures look to the team to make decisions or, when the leader must make the decision or take action, he or she will typically ask for the team's input.

Conflict generally results in collaborative and shared problem solving. Members will work toward discovering what the person or group wants and accommodate it. Keeping the peace is important. Clashes occur when someone is upset about not being included; angry over not being heard; feeling ignored; not being invited to participate and feel a part of something; and the perception that someone is putting self-interest ahead of the team's interest and performance.

Among the approaches to *incentive and reward*, those that best align to and reinforce group and team contribution are shared reward, equity, team recognition, and social celebrations. Often, social celebrations have a greater affect than shared monetary rewards. A high degree of value is placed on recognition that an individual is a member of, or is identified with, a team that performs well. For this reason, employee-owned companies with shared reward systems perform well when aligned with the participation preference.

When it comes to *hiring*, group involvement in the interview and decision making processes are keys to success. One aspect of hiring well, and often the primary concern of the participation culture, is finding the person who offers the best interpersonal fit with the other members of the team. Group interviews often provide the opportunity for a hiring team to experience the candidate together.

Role definition in the participation culture usually centers on being a team player and the ability to work well with teammates. Getting along is important, as is the ability to work cross-functionally. When it comes to development, a great deal of emphasis is placed on knowing what other members of the team do, what the required skills are, and concern for the other team members. When a team member goes off for training, that person is generally expected to share what is learned.

When it comes to *customer interface*, John's company is a great example. Cross-functional teams work directly with the customers they serve and spend time with them. Through a natural extension of the culture, the customer is often the center of focus or considered "one of us." Emphasis is placed on relationships and knowing the customer well. This sense of bonding and connection creates a foundation for long-term trusted relationships. The overriding qualities of the customer interface are connection, community, and attention.

Teamwork is all about involvement and looking out for one another. When groups in a participation culture are performing at their best, communication is informal and free flowing. Much as in John's company, this applies to how team members work with one another, as well as how teams across the company communicate and work with one another. Self-directed workgroups and teams can also succeed in a participation culture.

The *structure* of participation-preference cultures consist of relatively flat hierarchies comprised of cross-functional teams. Team leaders are assigned. Shared leadership can also work well, and while teams have direct supervision, it may appear that leaders are responsible for multiple teams. One aspect of cultures and their structures that is often overlooked is the environment in which they work. To support interaction and informal communication, participation cultures are generally partial to open workspaces and environments. In John's company, the lunchroom is used as an open space, inviting dialogue and information sharing. The outdoor picnic and recreation area reinforces group identity and employee cohesiveness. The company culture communicates "we."

The twelfth culture key is *aligned values*. How words are defined offers insight. Some words that are consistently used to define the values of a participation-preference culture include teamwork, family, listening, community, respect for the individual, equality, cooperation, fairness, collaboration, diversity, and inclusive.

Harley-Davidson has a set of values that demonstrate the alignment of its culture's values to the values it communicates to its customers. "We ride with our customers" is the statement that defines the company's customer-centric approach, which is based on deep emotional connections. In aligning its culture, the company puts a great degree of value on its team-based collaborative approach and the inclusivity of its diverse workforce. The company's stated values include telling the truth; keeping our promises; respecting the individual; encouraging intellectual curiosity; and, being fair. The company's participation preference is obvious.

Disney prides itself on its teamwork and inclusive culture, particularly in its theme park business. That isn't lost on the over 70 million visitors it attracts every year. When a company is aligned, it creates a strong force of attraction.

THE EXPERTISE PREFERENCE

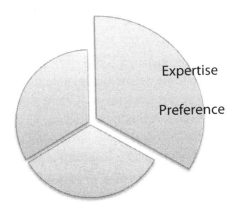

The management term "up or out," supposedly originates from the idea that a company should hire the most talented people it can find, give them an opportunity to learn and grow, prove themselves, and eventually become key assets of the company. Sometimes, the reward is becoming an owner or shareholder in the company. For example, in professional service companies—accounting, engineering and law, for example—one hires the best and offers them the prospect, within a designated timeline, to become a partner of the firm. If the person fails to perform at the required level, they are asked to leave. The idea is pretty straightforward. This exemplifies the expertise preference culture.

The motivation is for the employee to become an expert, building his or her capabilities, and becoming as competent as possible. Power and influence is derived by achieving status and ranking at the top of one's peer group. The better one performs, the more other group members are challenged and given the opportunity to advance.

Imagine a company with over 12,000 employees, all vying for the chance to consistently be among the best at their craft. Based on their competency and specialty areas, employees are assigned to projects that are run by well-qualified project managers who possess a clear set of capabilities and the know-how that best aligns to customer needs. The company prides itself on being able to address the customer's most challenging problems. The greater the problem, the more the company will show its determination and passion to perform. As a result, it attracts some of the brightest people. It is known for leveraging their intellect and thinking, constantly and relentlessly challenging them to be their best, to achieve as much as they can.

In alignment to customer motivation, the company sees itself as a preeminent institution. It prides itself on building the capabilities of its people at every level. Teams are built by assembling a collection of the best talent available. Those who have proven themselves and earned their place in the company are trusted with ranking other employees and assigning them to wherever they will have the best opportunity for learning and development. The emphasis is on constantly challenging and growing people to be the best they can be. The expression that is used to describe the company's culture is "grow or go."

The company I'm describing is McKinsey and Company, a global management consulting firm whose culture displays a clear preference for expertise. Its reputation is built on the depth of its industry and functional competency. It is a model for optimization of determination, influence, and the application of knowledge. It is also very well aligned.

The underlying traits and characteristics that makes it so extraordinary are the same traits that make Samsung, Wal-Mart, Apple, IKEA, and Toyota great companies—a preference for expertise.

In expertise cultures, *power and influence* are gained through the ability of the individual to demonstrate competencies and skills. Employees advance based on how well they compare with their peers—their rankings in the hierarchy. With advancement, comes a position and role of authority.

In less formal expertise cultures, it's not always about the authority that's granted through position or title nor is there as much dependence on hierarchy. It is more subtle and more about one's aptitude and abilities, yet the power and influence still goes to those considered the best and the brightest.

Those who demonstrate the highest level of expertise do the *planning and goal setting*, yet this doesn't mean that it is left only to individuals. Often, it is left to committees that, much like project teams, are comprised of those thought to offer the experience and knowledge to best create them. Membership in such committees is usually earned and determined by those with established authority. Regardless of longevity, when a person is no longer seen as sufficiently competent or as contributing significant knowledge or expertise, he or she is typically removed from the team. In many companies, the leader has the authority to create the vision and plan the future. In fact, often employees expect the leader to provide the direction and plan for the company or team.

In expertise cultures, the term "individual contributor" is often used, conveying the focus on individual goals and outcomes. In some instances, individuals are asked to define their own goals. In others, the supervisor, manager, or leader defines them. Sometimes the employee is asked to produce his or her own goals and a plan to achieve them, while the leader separately yet simultaneously does the same thing. Then, they meet and agree on a set of goals that incorporates both perspectives.

This construct can be applied on a larger scale and used for an entire company's planning and goal setting. Groups or teams throughout the company define their particular set of goals and plans, and then meet to agree on the companywide plan and outcomes. Often the process includes members from the different areas or groups who challenge each other and look for ways to improve the individual plans. This process is known as a "roll up," because the individual parts of the planning are done independently and then rolled up into one companywide strategy or plan.

In relation to leading and managing change, expertise cultures work best when individuals are change champions and teams are change initiators. Because of the natural energy of people within the culture to want constant advancement, there is an organic element of change and, because the culture reinforces the competitive nature of the individual, there is a natural propensity for creativity and innovation. The expertise culture is the ideal place for self-starters and people who want to be their best, to be challenged and grow, and to work in a passionate and creative environment. This offers an opportunity for anyone to step up, take ownership of their own future, and perform to the highest potential. All of this provides the fuel for change and innovation.

When it comes to *problem solving*, the best and brightest people are relied on to solve problems; often the highest performing employees are the "go-to" resources and enjoy the reputation of creating solutions and answers to the most pressing or difficult problems. Unlike a participation culture, where teams and groups are brought together to solve problems, expertise cultures engage only those who need to be involved—people with the specific skills and competencies to solve the problem or have the authority to make things happen. Members of participative cultures enjoy meetings; members of expertise cultures avoid them. Unless there is a personal benefit, meetings can often be seen as a waste of time and a distraction from getting work done.

Decision making is generally top-down or content specific. When it is content specific, decisions are left to those with the greatest knowledge, expertise, and know-how. Often, a leader calls on the expert to come up with solutions and make recommendations, and then makes the decision. Because the ongoing nature of the culture promotes individual performance and accomplishment, some of the best decisions come from people challenging one another; the company or team benefits from the creative thinking that evolves from it. In most expertise preference companies, the influence on decision making and the decisions themselves are made from the top, even when a company is very large. In some instances, the culture supports a militaristic approach to decisions. At Samsung, a company of close to 370,000 employees, the direction and decision making comes from the top and directives are closely followed. This cascades through the organization and is reflected in how most problems are addressed and how decisions are made.

When *managing conflict*, expertise cultures typically like a good argument; people enjoy challenging each other's positions, thereby creating an environment that promotes digging deeper into a problem and applying logic and data to reach the best outcome. Argument is based on fact, logic, and sound reasoning; it is not driven by emotion. A participation culture seeks common ground and collaborates to find the "we"; expertise cultures lean toward the "I." Resolutions to conflict are achieved by finding the right answer, and the tendency is for people to want to be right. Conflicts are also resolved by the leader, who has the authority to step in and decide the issue.

Another way we can differentiate culture preferences surrounding disagreement and conflict is by tracing the origin of the conflict to the key emotional influencers of the culture. In a participation culture, conflict mostly begins when people feel left out or ignored. In expertise culture, it originates from issues about who is right and wrong, about whether people have had the opportunity to demonstrate their competencies and capabilities. It is about who has individual authority, and how that authority is used.

This insight also applies to how conflict is best managed. Participation cultures prefer group involvement. In expertise cultures, individual challenge and argument serves best. One is not better than the other. It's a matter of how it aligns to the preference of the culture and the predictability it offers its members. Dealing with conflict is difficult not just because we fear that our needs won't be met, which is the most important aspect. Often, it is also because we fear the consequences and outcomes we'll be contributing to if we fail. In expertise cultures, the message when someone falters, missteps, or makes mistakes is to recover quickly, learn from your mistake, and try not to do it again. If you don't, you won't be there much longer. Although the culture expresses the idea that taking risks is good, if the actions of its leaders are misaligned, the message is lost and employees fear taking chances.

Many of the lessons about the values and beliefs of the culture, the rules of how people engage and interact, and what is acceptable and unacceptable behavior are learned by observing how people manage conflicts. Employees who have a clear idea of a culture's expectations for managing conflicts appreciate the predictability and feel empowered. In expertise cultures, where the emphasis is on competence, this is vital.

The primary approach to *incentive and reward* in an expertise culture is individual: pay-for-performance, competency-based pay and status, promotion and rank, and tying reward directly to the outcomes of the employee's efforts. Individual recognition is a source of motivation. One company I worked with created a technical "hall of fame," with companywide recognition going to those who made the most significant and innovative contributions to its technology. Another aspect of incentive and rewards are what we commonly refer to as "perks": company-funded travel, vacations and holidays, flexible working hours, club memberships, professional development opportunities, and assorted personal favors. Although a goal of expertise cultures, in general, is to directly connect compensation to performance and achievement, discretionary rewards and perks often reflect the preferences of leaders to reward those who best serve their own goal attainment and personal success. (Note: This is not unique to expertise cultures, and you should pay particular attention to it.)

Hiring in expertise cultures, like McKinsey and Company's, is generally competency focused. The process centers on finding and hiring the person with the best skill, knowledge, and aptitude for the job. Compared with participation cultures, which look for the best team and interpersonal fit, the expertise culture puts greater value on first finding the right set of competencies and worries less about culture fit. In some instances, strict adherence to policy and procedure is followed; in others, experts recruit people with the expertise they need and then concern themselves with what is required to hire them.

For example, I coached a company leader who meets with people who have specific competencies and appear to be an excellent fit for his company's culture. He then finds a position or creates an opportunity for them. He sees it as one of his critical competencies. Although he does this outside the company's normal hiring process, he has had such a high degree of success, it has become an accepted norm.

Orientation in an expertise culture focuses on policies and procedures and getting the newcomer to work and contribute as quickly as possible. The message often is "Welcome. Show us what you can do." In contrast, in participation cultures, the emphasis is on getting to know everyone and learning how to fit into the team.

Role definition is highly oriented to leveraging abilities, skills, and know-how. For this reason, expertise cultures are organized into functional areas and teams, which allow for the predictable application of specialties and increased efficiency. Great emphasis is on how people can best apply their skills to their roles and their titles, such as test technician, marketing specialist, account manager, reflect this. For consultants, McKinsey uses role definitions and titles, such as specialist, expert, and senior expert, which are forms of organization, competency recognition, and level of position power.

Customer interface is left to those who demonstrate that specific competency, and most expertise cultures organize functionally to meet the product or service requirements considered to be most important in conveying value and brand intention. Often this results in functionally oriented customer service teams, where those with the highest level of customer management proficiency are in roles that best respond to the customer's needs.

Apple's retail stores are excellent examples of how role definition, brand intention, culture, and customer experience are aligned. Apple's stores are organized by product competency and aligned role definitions. As we've seen, the customer is greeted by an employee whose role it is to direct customers to the person with the specific product knowledge they need. Because Apple sells preeminent products, this approach offers a high degree of alignment with customer motivation. Those with the highest degree of competency get to work in the roles with the highest level of status and respect—the genius bar.

Teamwork has a functional or project focus. The emphasis is on bringing together individual competency to leverage group performance. When teams are functionally oriented, how well a team can focus on a particular part of the whole is key. This can apply to an operational element of a company or a specific part of how a product or service is created and delivered. It requires meeting the contradictory challenge of simultaneously separating parts while bringing them together. This is a challenge for all cultures. However, it is especially true for expertise cultures.

Because functional teaming is challenging, companies are increasingly adapting and applying variations of project, program, and ad hoc teaming, which some expertise cultures refer to as cross-functional teaming. Whatever label you use, it's a matter of aligning everyone to how it works and what their part is in making it work successfully. This can happen in formal or informal ways.

The more formal approaches to program and project teaming include the process of project planning, which includes defining roles, identifying the required knowledge and skill sets, and then assigning people to fill the roles and deliver the required outcomes. This approach lends itself well to both breaking down some of the silos attributed to expertise cultures and better utilizing talent.

The other approach encourages people to seek out one another across functional boundaries, practice areas, and the various centers of competency. Unplanned and impromptu teaming is an aspect of high-performing companies that translates into greater speed, collaboration, information sharing, and the culture values of agility and empowerment. It also results in higher levels of transparency and trust across different parts of the company. For this reason, it's always worth exploring further. This is particularly true for expertise cultures.

How people team depends on structure. Expertise cultures most often *structure* in ways that emphasize the coming together of functionality and hierarchy. The organization of how things get done and who does them directly reflects the emphasis on competency and expertise. To further leverage these traits and to align to the goal of increased collaboration and communication, companies are increasingly using formal matrix designs and structures, resulting in improved cross-functional work processes that can incorporate program and project teaming and increase the opportunity for informal and unplanned teaming.

The *aligned values* of expertise cultures can be described using words such as challenging, expertise, analytical, innovative, superior, excellence, world-class, preeminent, solutions-oriented, leading edge, quality, high-performing, entrepreneurial, fast-paced, unique, accountability, mastery, teamwork, integrity, professionalism, achieving, and personal excellence. These describe the shared values that are common to expertise-preference cultures. For them to become shared values, as demonstrated through intentional action, requires a clear definition and alignment to what the company does, why it does it, and how it does it. Without that clarity and alignment, they are just words.

THE AUTHENTICITY PREFERENCE

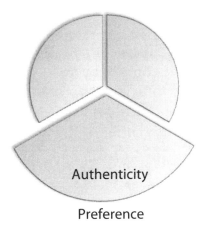

Some words, such as love, truth, peace, compassion, and freedom, that describe the human experience don't immediately connect to most definitions of company culture because they don't resonate with our everyday connection to the products or services we buy. Yet, we notice them when they are missing and tend to try to find our way back to them. Why? Because it's natural for us to be inspired to connect and work together for the wellness of our shared humanity.

Several years ago, my wife and I and our four children found ourselves in an open Colorado field preparing to spend the night in a small shelter built from cardboard boxes. We were a part of a larger group that had come together to support a not-for-profit named Invisible Children, whose mission is to stop Joseph Kony and Lord's Resistance Army from abducting, killing, and displacing civilians in East and Central Africa. For decades Kony has been the target of an immense manhunt involving a collaborative effort of four African armies and the U.S. military.

Over a period of thirty years, Kony has killed thousands of civilians and is said to have abducted over 25,000 young boys, who are indoctrinated into Kony's army as child soldiers.

At the event, we briefly experienced what life as a displaced family was like, eating saltine crackers for lunch, dinner, and breakfast. The women and girls stood in long lines to get a small amount of water, and we slept on the ground. We were engaging in a shared experience of empathy and compassion.

Fast-forward several years to a conference room in Dubai. I was invited by Legatum, a global private investment group that allocates capital to businesses and organizations that sustain human development, to share my work and engage in a conversation about alignment. Along with an exceptional history of asset management, the group members have a shared commitment to the distribution of capital to fund and support extraordinary humanitarian efforts and worldwide economic development. Legatum passionately supports entrepreneurship and provides the stewardship required to assure its longer term success.

Several years ago, in the support of a not-for-profit working to protect innocent children, they funded a documentary titled *Invisible Children*. It was the film that captivated my family and led to our participation. When I entered the conference room in Dubai, I did not know the connection. Legatum is a wonderful example of a global business that provides insight into the characteristics of an authenticity-preference culture. When an authenticity culture is in alignment, it demonstrates an intention to aspire to a set of higher ideals. It undertakes goals that convey a sense of purpose that can lift the human spirit and then achieves them. In authenticity cultures, *power and influence* is gained by demonstrating a commitment to the company's values, higher ideals, and mission. Those who interact with others in charismatic and inspiring ways often have the greatest influence. It is not about being the best, the brightest, or the friendliest; it is about being genuine, being authentic, and engaging others. Being optimistic and positive, as well as showing compassion and empathy, generally result in the ability to have an effect on others.

Planning and goal setting is centered on the values and beliefs of what is possible and best delivers to the cause. Participation in planning is most often group based; there is a sense of community in how people come together to agree on goals. A shared sense of purpose and an organic process is not an unusual way for an authenticity culture to strategize. Methods similar to open space and blue sky are planning and goal-setting approaches that are value driven and aim at building mutually satisfying outcomes are common to authenticity cultures, conveying an "anything is possible" attitude.

Problem solving is focused on the intention of the group and often involves open dialogue about what solutions may work. Subjective and intuitive approaches are considered and often given as much or greater attention than more analytically based ideas. Group members expect one another to be open to sharing and hearing each other's ideas, thereby promoting creativity and provoking imaginative thought. In an authenticity culture, employees are welcome to contribute insights and ideas, regardless how "out of the box" they may seem.

Decision making is often influenced by ethical and moral considerations and filtering decisions through the lens of whether they align with what the right thing to do is. How a decision aligns to the core values and beliefs of the group is more important than its measurable financial or performance outcome. Finding alignment between the two offers the best alternative. Everyone has a voice and the intention is for every person to be heard.

An example of this is an alternative elementary school, which at its founding adopted an inclusive governing model that centered on a unanimous decision-making process. At first, it posed a risk to many who had been involved in parent groups that had relied on majority-based decisions and voting. Over time, the teachers, parents, and community members found the openness and honesty empowering and discovered that accessible dialogue lessened the politics associated with the governing of a school. As with any culture, there were parents and teachers who chose not to stay. In a relatively short period of time, the community became aligned.

Over two decades later, Horizons K-8 in Boulder, Colorado, still uses the same decision-making model. Before every meeting, the decision-making process is reviewed to remind everyone of how things get done and of the values that provide the foundation for the methods and processes the culture engages in.

In an authenticity culture, *disagreements and conflicts* are usually dealt with openly. While individuals typically are rigid in protecting the company's values and ideals and its definition of the right thing, members of authenticity cultures pride themselves on self-awareness and flexibility. Conflict resolution generally meets the needs of the parties involved and is often perceived as an opportunity to further develop the relationships of those involved, including feelings of intimacy and trust. A great degree of emphasis is placed on genuineness and honesty. Open expression of thoughts and feelings is expected; employees who are perceived as disingenuous or withholding typically find themselves in jeopardy.

In authenticity cultures, *incentives and rewards* are intrinsic and members are motivated more by the company's purpose and values. L'Occitane is a good example. Employees at the store level are not high-income earners, yet they take pride in connecting with customers and taking care of them. A high degree of alignment exists between the individual employee and the customer motivation for caring. The company also places value on caring for its employees and encourages a sense of service that creates an emotional thread that connects leadership, the culture, the employee, and the customer. L'Occitane has a very well aligned authenticity culture.

Another form of reward in an authenticity culture is personal development and self-actualization. Because the culture honors self-expression and openness, the opportunity for personal growth and the pursuit of one's professional and personal passions are great motivators.

Hiring is highly intentional and decisions are based primarily on how prospective employees connect to the company's purpose and culture. Of the three cultures, authenticity cultures have the easiest time finding the right fits probably because of the attraction of the company's purpose and the highly intuitive aspects of its culture. Often, there is an immediate connection with new hires similar to when kindred spirits meet. While this can happen in participation and expertise cultures, it is less likely that a person, especially a new hire, would express it as freely.

The criterion that authenticity cultures rely on in their hiring is the alignment of an individual's sense of purpose and personal preference for being forthright and open. In working together, this means being caring and considerate and building relationships that are open and honest. This shared quality further aligns to how the customer is treated and the willingness of employees to help one another. This sincerity is conveyed to and reinforced when a new member joins the group. Much as the participation culture helps newcomers feel included and an expert culture invites them to show their competency, the authenticity culture conveys acceptance.

These qualities show in how authenticity cultures approach *role definition*. A sense of individual empowerment allows people to pursue that which best satisfies the immediate fulfillment of the company's purpose. Zappos, the online shoe company, is a good example. From the outset, employees were encouraged and empowered to choose and take on any role to do what was needed to deliver happiness to the customer. This meant that someone in an IT role could jump in to fill orders or stock inventory. This dedicated and value-centric culture allows team members to help and mentor one another. There is always a risk that self-interest can get in the way of fulfilling the obligations of their assigned role, whereas in an authenticity culture, there is greater emphasis on not letting one another down. Because there's an ongoing concern about being able to say no, employees are more likely to help when asked, even when they are stretched.

Bruce Lish of Blue Diamond Almonds, whom I introduced you to at the beginning of this chapter, is another good example. Bruce filled various positions throughout his career, stepping into different roles as the company and situation required. His goal was to serve the company and those around him. While his roles were formally defined, he was free to contribute in the manner that best responded to the company's mission, purpose, and culture.

When it comes to *customer interface*, the same ethos applies. Customers are to be connected with and cared for. In an authenticity culture, regardless of an employee's position or role, everyone is empowered to provide service. This empowerment allows employees to make the decisions necessary to achieve customer satisfaction. In participation cultures, the customer's satisfaction is measured by how attentively they are treated; in an expertise culture, on how competently the customer's needs are met; and in authenticity cultures by how well mutual benefit and trust are achieved.

Teamwork comes fairly naturally to authenticity cultures. The key motivation is shared ideals and values. Individual teams are often empowered to take responsibility for their own planning and goal setting, which can include the team's definition of its mission and strategic vision. One might think that this would result in multiple teams with misaligned goals and strategies, yet this rarely happens in authenticity cultures. A good example is Whole Foods. In going store to store, most customers wouldn't even notice that the employees write the mission statements posted on the blackboards at each location. That's the strength of Whole Foods' authenticity culture, its mission, and shared ideals.

At Whole Foods, the commitment of its employees to the company's mission and culture supports why Whole Foods can successfully *structure* its employees into self-directed work teams. Authenticity cultures are able to engage in unique structures. The more the structure organically aligns to the flow of how the product or service is created and delivered, the easier it is for employees to leverage their empowerment. As a result, a company may find itself using a hybrid of structure options. This is a natural way authenticity cultures express themselves.

The *aligned values* that are common to authenticity cultures include inspiring, values-driven, caring, values-centered, integrity, truth, transparency, generosity, creative, uplifting, self-expression, actualizing, spirituality, positive, realizing, optimistic, faith, and love, among others.

ALIGNING THE IDEAL CULTURE

When it comes to defining a company's unique culture, along with the 12 culture keys, there are other characteristics to be considered. These include meetings, performance management practices, training and development, time-off and employee leave policy, attire, employee discipline, tuition and education assistance, employee communication, information technology, and the processes and tools used in measuring, reporting, and assessing performance results. Based on these and others, you can determine what characteristics best align to and serve the company. Whatever is in the best interest of alignment, with few exceptions, is in the best interest of the business.

It is the pursuit of such alignment that results in the linking of a company's culture to the needs of the customer. As the Figure 9.1 shows, extraordinary companies have brand intentions that align to the three customer motivations, six brand intentions, and three preferences of culture.

When you look at how the customer, brand intention, and culture come together, it becomes obvious that success requires that the company align with the emotional thread that runs through the three preferences. This connection motivates the customer and encourages employ-

Human Motivation	Customer Motivation	Brand Intention	Culture Preference
To feel important	Attention	Community	Participation
		Customization	
To feel competent	Competency	Preeminence	Expertise
		Low Price	
To feel accepted	Caring	Physical Wellbeing	Authenticity
		Personal Actualization	

Figure 9.1 The Ideal Culture

ees to work together in a manner that is aligned to customer needs and brings the brand intention to life in a way that results in the customer's trust. A company's culture brings this to life.

The next question is what does an ideal culture look like. To begin with, all three culture preferences can result in high-performing companies, so no one approach is better than another. Assuming a company's culture preference is aligned to its brand intention, how things get done internally is aligned to the external experience and meaning for the customer. For leaders, as well for its members, a company's unique approach to its culture's preference provides insight into the psychological and emotional threads that connect it to its mission and purpose, its customers, and its brand intention.

There is no one size fits all approach. The highest performing cultures are those with a clearly defined preference that also integrate traits and characteristics of the other two. To be successful, the preference and specific makeup of the culture must be clearly articulated.

As examples:

- At the team and company level, Whole Foods integrates elements of expertise in how it tracks and measures performance results and uses self-directed work teams to integrate ongoing participation into its authenticity culture.
- SAP uses online communities of practice, forums, and project teaming to integrate participation into its expertise culture.
- McKinsey and Company relies on strict adherence to standards of ethics and transparency to bring elements of authenticity to its expertise culture. It uses a matrix structure to integrate participation.
- Blue Diamond has a keen focus on quality and food safety, incorporating elements of expertise into its authenticity culture. Employees work in cross-functional teams, share roles, and participate in line dancing during breaks to integrate participation.
- The team at Decision Point Associates engages in high levels of communication to assure it delivers expertise in its tailored solutions. Its value for human life and safety integrate authenticity.
- Legatum has a clear value for high-level results that challenge employees and the group, integrating aspects of expertise into its authenticity culture.
- Teams at Harley-Davidson incorporate quality assurance methods, integrating expertise into its participative culture.

These examples demonstrate how aspects of two cultures are used in the service of company cultures. When introducing and integrating specific strategies and ideas, it's important to realize how relatively easy it is to cause confusion. For this reason, when strategizing how to best align a company's unique culture, there are four considerations. First, take great care in aligning to the business strategy. Be very intentional about it; it's easy to drift and dilute a culture. When this happens and the company again changes direction, the starts and stops and inconsistencies leave employees wondering if they're facing another "flavor of the month," if they know what they're doing, and whether they can trust the culture to be predictable.

Second, make sure that all leaders are in alignment with one another. If they are not, employees will sense the conflict, see the lack of commitment, and lose confidence in the culture, as well as in their leaders. The company also runs the risk of groups and teams disagreeing and finding themselves in conflict with one another.

Third, leverage culture to create change. In psychology, one approach to change is known as paradoxical intervention. Much like reverse psychology, in organizational or group contexts, this approach suggests using an already present aspect of group behavior to achieve the change being sought. For example, if a participation-culture team needs to increase a specific area of expertise or competency, instead of hiring a new member, the leader brings the issue to the members of the team and asks them to decide how to increase its capability, thereby leveraging the team's alignment to group problem solving and decision making.

Another example is a group of leaders of functional areas within an expertise culture struggling to communicate and collaborate. Rather than putting them in a room and expecting them to engage one another, the leader addresses each individual and sets personal expectations for their behavior to become more aligned with how things are to get done. Adding individual measurement and a feedback mechanism adds to the likelihood of success, as would personal leadership coaching that aims at the interpersonal and collaboration skills the individual needs to develop.

Assessing how well each works with the others and observing and measuring their overall improvement is a means of challenging each person. This is one of the reasons executive coaching and 360-feedback tools are used as much as they are in expertise cultures. The path to creating a better collaboration begins with a focus on improving the individual. If the team does engage in teambuilding activities and exercises, it's important to make sure the training aligns to the culture. Nothing is worse that a team spending time and energy learning team skills and processes that do not align to the culture and won't used.

Living in Colorado, I've facilitated a good deal of outdoor teambuilding. For teambuilding to work, it has to align to the culture in which the team operates. If I were to tell an expertise preference group to plan how to get down a river together as quickly as possible, they will try to determine who the experts are, who should lead, how to distribute competencies (and who gets the weak players), and be somewhat reluctant to stay together. Even if I were to instruct them to wait for one another and try to stay together, their natural tendency is to create teams and race down the river. They may even sabotage one another in order to win.

It would be more beneficial to instruct them to organize into teams and have a race and, as part of the experience, ask them to explore what they can learn about their actions and how they can improve their teamwork. By the way, expertise teams also like to drive racecars around a track to see who is the fastest—and call it teambuilding.

If I ask a participative team to race down the river, they are likely to join forces and help each other navigate as successfully as possible. They might, for example, tie rafts to one another to assure their entire team floats down the river together, although they were asked to compete.

For an authenticity group, you might need a raft or two, kayaks, and tubes, and then empower to go down the river in the fashion that suits them best. The most important part of the exercise is at the end, when participants are asked to reflect on their journey and share their personal experience. Based on their new self-knowledge, they will likely describe how they can individually and collectively apply their learning to self-actualize and increase their contribution to what they do.

The fourth is a reminder that to be successful requires ongoing and clear communication. It is just too easy to go off course. Leaders have to consistently engage employees in an ongoing conversation about the company's culture, how its traits of preference align to its brand intention, and how it aligns to its customer.

Applying the framework for alignment provides leaders with additional insight into a host of challenges they typically encounter, including the "us versus them" effect of subcultures that are in misalignment, thereby allowing the leader to change the culture of the group or to integrate it into the rest of the business. Lastly, it provides a roadmap for planning that can lead to the alignment of human resource and organizational development practices, including approaches to teambuilding and leadership development.

SOME OTHER THINGS TO THINK ABOUT

When it comes to aligning culture, there are a few other risks. The first concerns *language and terminology*. As with any business framework or model, it's easy to use language that is unfamiliar or that does not align with how people actually communicate. When it comes to applying the Business Code and the traits and characteristics of culture preferences, leaders should use the language that is prevalent in a culture and pay particular attention to being clear and consistent about definitions and how they come to life as behaviors and norms. The term "collaboration" is commonly used across all three culture preferences and across companies, yet the definition varies. That being said, whenever new terminology is introduced, it's important to define what it means.

All cultures will have stories. Be aware of them; they tell you a great deal about the culture and its artifacts, values, and beliefs. In defining and creating clarity, a culture's stories offer leaders wonderful opportunities to connect with the norms and values of a culture. They also help employees connect with and better understand a culture's preference and uniqueness.

When a company discovers or intentionally pursues multiple brand intentions and market strategies, examine the consequence on the alignment of that strategy to the culture. It is much easier when the strategies are aligned. A good example is Toyota and Lexus. One of the reasons this has worked so well is that both brand intentions are aligned with the company's expertise culture. Another is Harley-Davidson's strategy to offer customized motorcycles. Because both community and customization are aligned with the company's participation culture, the likelihood of success is greatly increased. Furthermore, the culture and brand intentions are aligned to the customer motivation and provide the common emotional thread that gives the brand and customer experience its power of trust.

In working with companies considering new brand intentions or customer strategies, I always suggest exploring how it affects the company's alignment. One option that has served many companies well is to establish a separate group or team, with a separate subculture that aligns with the brand intention. This requires diligence and commitment. Leaders, like the rest of us, tend to want everything to look and feel alike.

Alignment is a very valuable asset when considering mergers and acquisitions. Much like when companies fail by pursuing a strategy that doesn't align to their cultures, the rate of failure for mergers and acquisitions is astounding. Most studies and experts put the failure rate at 70 percent or higher. One of the major factors, perhaps the major factor, is an inability to integrate cultures.

Using the Business Code and alignment as the tool for due diligence and strategizing brings great value to the process. There are four reasons to engage in a merger or acquisition. The first is to bring companies together to increase shareholder value. If that's the only reason, you risk not getting there unless the cultures align. Some barriers to alignment usually surface, and some can cause big problems, both strategically and financially.

The second is to buy or combine market share. Unless it's a commodity and people don't care where it comes from, if the cultures don't align and the customer experience isn't the same, the customers will be disappointed and spend their money elsewhere.

The third reason is to deliver increased operational capability. While this is all about integrating systems, processes, and technology, if the cultures are not aligned, success can be achieved only if the employees of only one of the companies are needed. Yet even this is not easy because much of the success in applying systems, processes, technology, and the like relies on the skills, knowledge, and competencies of the people who run them. Lose the people, and you may lose significant value.

The fourth reason is to buy technology or the competencies and talents of people, which often come together. In this scenario, if the cultures of the companies don't align, if you're just buying the intellectual property and don't need the people, the merger or acquisition has a better chance of working. Yet, even then, you may run into situations where people in the acquiring company are resistant to the new technology or the customer is not interested. If it is all about the competencies, knowledge, and skills of the people and the cultures do not align, it's likely not to get the desired results.

The Business Code provides a great vantage point from which to better predict whether an M&A will result in success or failure. While the three culture preferences afford the opportunity to assess the alignment and misalignment of two companies and their cultures, it's still important to delve deeply into the details of each culture. Two companies may have the same culture, yet each is unique. In searching for those unique qualities and nuances, you may find misalignments in traits and characteristics

e and overcome. For this reason, the twelve
he due diligence and assessment process.
lications of the Business Code to the align-
a clear path to strategizing the alignment
on and culture to the customer is one of its
ll consider the fourth element of The Business

ap.

Aligning Leadership

Role Modeling, Reinforcement, Reputation

WHAT WE EXPECT OF LEADERS

A couple months ago, on a plane waiting to take off from London to New York, the passenger next to me introduced herself. Her name was Rosemary. She sold electrical parts and was headed to New Jersey to meet with a perspective supplier. She asked what I did, and I told her. "I know plenty of people who could use your help," she laughed. "I get that a lot," I told her. "Most people know someone they think should be talking to me—usually their boss." After a brief pause, she leaned over and quietly said, "He drives me crazy—*absolutely* crazy." "Really? How?," I asked. "Well, for starters, he can never make his mind up about anything. Everything is always last minute. The world and the industry is changing around us, yet he's not doing anything about it. He has no direction. I don't know what he's thinking. I don't think he's thinking at all. It's scary. It's really scary. I'm not sure what to do about it. I've been thinking a lot about it. I'm thinking about looking for another job, but at my age, and as a woman in my industry, it's not easy."

"Have you talked to him about it?," I asked. Rosemary shook her head. "It may be a good start. You may get answers to some of your questions."

After a long pause, she said, "I don't think I can do that. He's likely to tell me something I don't want to hear."

Leaders influence people's emotions. Sometimes they do it without even realizing it. Great leaders are those who are aware and conscious of their influence. They encourage people to deeply connect to what is most meaningful in their lives and bring it into being. The really great ones influence people to be themselves, to pursue their dreams and possibilities, and to be their best at everything they do, although on the surface it may not seem that way.

I've worked with leaders for quite some time and, like the rest of us, experienced leadership all my life. They have all influenced the way we see ourselves and our resulting decisions and actions. Some have influenced us more than others, leaving lasting impressions and, in some instances, changed the course of our lives.

Sometimes leaders influence and lead with intention, consciously engaging others. Others do it unconsciously, unintentionally influencing and swaying us. Rosemary's boss was probably unaware that his influence was affecting her emotions and making her anxious and worried about the future and less confident in him as a leader.

The role of the leader is very powerful. As a result, it is important for leaders to always pay attention to their actions. One wonders, does the CEO of Rosemary's company have a vision and strategy for the future? Is he communicating well enough and in a manner that deserves the commitment and engagement of his employees? Do they trust in his abilities? Do they trust him to be truthful with them? Do they trust enough in their relationships to engage in an honest conversation with him? Rosemary is too fearful to have an open and honest dialogue with him. There is an incredible level of interest and a significant body of work devoted to the topic of leadership and how and why leadership works. This information is important and provides great insight into the nature of leaders and those who follow them. When the influence of leadership scales, it is amazing. I am often surprised that a large group of people will consciously choose to give up its decision-making power. When it does, however, members expect a benefit in return.

I've concluded that we expect three things of great leaders: *to create change, pursue truth, and know themselves. As the result of doing these well, leaders influence people to deeply connect to what is most meaningful to their lives and bring it into being. They influence others to live life to their fullest capability.*

It's hard for leaders to accomplish any of the three without accomplishing the other two. Some examples of their interdependence follow. To create change one must know the current reality and the truth (often referred to as clarity) about what one is trying to achieve. If a leader does not know how he responds to change, it's difficult to create it. Without knowing himself, it's hard to step into a conflict to seek the truth. To influence others to change, leaders have to know their own truth.

WHAT DOES THIS HAVE TO DO WITH BUSINESS?

So far, we've explored human motivation and how our needs translate into and align to the three customer motivations; the six brand intentions, connecting the "what" and the "why"; and the ways products or services are strategically branded and sold. We also explored the three preferences of culture and the richness and power of *how* we work with one another, using the Business Code as the framework to understand the importance of alignment to any company or team. Now, we will examine the fourth element of alignment, leadership.

Most often leaders establish cultures based on their perceptions of how things ought to be. Very often, the cultures of companies and teams take on the traits and characteristics of their leaders, and we can often observe that the preferences of the culture are in alignment to the preferences—the style—of the leader.

At the most basic level, leaders influence culture in three ways; I call them the three Rs. They are role modeling, reinforcement, and reputation. The following equation is an easy way to remember them and see how they come together:

Role Modeling + Reinforcement = Reputation

In a company or team, *leaders are the role models* for how people are expected to work with one another to create success. Through their behavior, leaders provide the context for what is appropriate and inappropriate and what is acceptable and unacceptable behavior. In practice, this means it is not what you say that matters most; it is what you do. Actions speak louder than words. If a leader's actions and behavior are misaligned, how can they expect their followers not to be? This alignment of the leader is the seed of personal responsibility and how expectations are eventually met. Responsibility means keeping commitments. Accountability is how we measure the degree to which we are responsible, consistent, and forthright in keeping our promises. If the leader is not responsible or accountable, people's expectations will not be met.

Leaders are also responsible for *reinforcing* what behavior is acceptable and unacceptable and how people are intended to act toward and work with one another. This requires the leader to be actively engaged. Leaders reinforce behavior and how things are done in two distinct ways: *active reinforcement* and *passive reinforcement*. The first occurs when a leader is able to recognize what creates success in the culture and actively engages in reinforcing that behavior. For example, the leader sees someone, or a group of people, acting in the manner that is wanted in the culture, and actively reinforces it by talking about it, complimenting it, or rewarding the behavior and its outcomes.

The other side of active reinforcement is recognizing and confronting negative behavior and actions. This is creating change by expressing the truth. I define "confront" as stepping into the truth. To seek the truth, one has to be willing to step into the situation and the conversation. Thus, active reinforcement of what is unacceptable requires the leader to consistently confront it.

Often, leaders reinforce passively, thereby missing the opportunity to positively reinforce what is expected and failing to confront what is unacceptable in which case the leader silently gives permission to and reinforces the negative behavior.

The sum of role modeling and reinforcement is the *reputation* of the leader, which provides insight into whether he or she is truly aligned. Whether one is running a small local business or leading a large multinational enterprise, it is hard to imagine that the reputation of the leader does not influence and resemble the reputation of the business. Reputation influences a company's culture, as well as the customer's perception. Steve Jobs's reputation as the CEO of Apple is a great example. So powerful was the connection between his reputation and the company's that customers felt a kinship to him and believed that his personality was embedded in the innovation and quality of the products he oversaw. His reputation was so synonymous with Apple that the company's shareholder value was questioned and its culture cast in doubt when he died. This is clear evidence of how leadership is intimately and powerfully tied to culture.

Leaders build a number of paradigms about what a culture should be, including its core values, perceptions, concepts, and the resulting practices shared throughout the company. Leaders influence teams based on how they perceive the business environment and what it takes to succeed. Very often how groups and individual align to the pursuit of market and customer strategies are the direct reflection of how the leader thinks and feels about them. It's easy to see how leadership behavior misaligned to strategy may cause members to behave in a manner that does not support the brand intention of shared purpose.

Leadership influences the organization's and team's structure, how teaming occurs within, and across, workgroups. It also role models how company and team members communicate and how conflict is dealt within the culture. Leadership behavior misaligned to culture quickly results in distrust and lack of commitment among organization and team members, eventually negatively affecting performance. Among the most negative results are the shutting down of communication and the lack of information sharing, both of which occur when people fear the consequences of speaking up. Thus, the leader's issues become the company's issues.

The alignment of leadership behavior to the culture is essential. To better understand this, consider how human motivation that manifests itself through our behaviors influences how leaders think and act and how they influence others. What will quickly become apparent is leaders demonstrate a preference toward one of three leadership preferences and approaches—the one that reflects their individual personality and psychological makeup. This personal preference then becomes visible in the culture and, with few exceptions, a culture eventually develops and relies on a readily recognizable preference for the leadership that best aligns to it.

The three preferences of leadership are *participative, expert,* and *servant*. While leaders will at various times demonstrate qualities and characteristics of all three, their leadership approach provides consistency in their role modeling and reputation and a sense of reliability and predictability that others come to expect and that the culture will respond to in an aligned manner.

Through their preferences, leaders present patterns for how they communicate, make decisions, manage conflict, engage in competition, challenge others, run meetings, interface with customers, and manage risk. This is key to understanding why the behavior of the leader is often the greatest influence on the culture of the organization. When leadership at the top and throughout an organization is misaligned, it quickly results in confusion, a lack of predictability and trust, and dysfunctional conflict, all of which ultimately impact performance.

One of the most powerful aspects and opportunities of leadership development is enhancing self-knowledge and teaching leaders to choose the behavior that aligns with, role models, and reinforces the culture. Such power translates into consistency in the wide array of behaviors that people in organizations engage in, both individually and collectively, resulting in the consistent delivery of intention to the customer and the development and effective leadership of a well-aligned and high-performing culture.

One of the more powerful observations stemming from the application of aligned leadership is that a leader's orientation is also a reliable indicator of why individual leaders prefer a specific brand intention and how they pursue advancement and innovation. It also explains why partners and multiple leaders within an organization or team have differing views on the wide range of possibilities that relate to the basic what, why, and how of the business.

Individual preferences are what most often keeps executive and leadership teams from truly aligning. Frequently, the lack of a group's individual and collective self-knowledge interferes with team members coming together to agree on strategy, direction, and culture. When we pull back the layers and unfold the relationships, the emotions behind the challenges and issues inevitably get in the way of success.

THE THREE PREFERENCES OF LEADERS

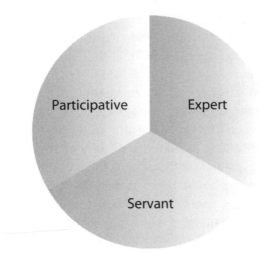

There are many ways to define the approaches and patterns of leadership. Most have great commonalities. I find defining leadership style through an individual's preference is consistent with how we actually choose our behavior and with the approach to alignment the Business Code offers.

The idea that leaders are better when they have self-knowledge is not new. Understanding your preference as a leader gives you knowledge about your behaviors and central tendencies and about how you influence others to take action. Understanding your behavior provides you with powerful insights. For one, you'll be better able to acknowledge your emotions and feelings. You'll gain an increased awareness of their origin in your own self-concept in relationship to the world. Your self-concept includes how you see yourself emotionally, physically, socially, and spiritually, as well as what your psychological needs and preferences are for importance, competency, and acceptance.

The result of our emotion and feelings are our behaviors. Self-knowledge about our behavior, what we do and say at any particular moment, allows us to connect our behavior though our emotions to what we seek from others. We all have the power of choice. We can choose what we do and what we say to influence others. As a leader with the power of choice you can be flexible in selecting the behavior that will best serve the relationship and your desired outcome.

It is important to remember that:

- There is no single preference or style of leadership behavior that is successful in all situations.
- While you possess a preference and orientation to your approach as a leader, you have the power to choose a specific set of behaviors in any given situation.
- Of the three primary styles of leadership, no one is better than the other two. Successful leaders are able to demonstrate leadership behaviors that reflect the environment or culture they are leading.
- Your leadership preference reflects the way you prefer to lead and describes "how" you and others see your general approach, as well as behaviors you choose specific to the different actions you undertake as a leader. Some behaviors and actions are directly related to your leadership and contribute to your overall make-up as a leader. It is important to consider the specific elements of leadership that you may apply in different situations.
- Your overall leadership behavior is not completely defined by your preference; it is a unique combination of behaviors and leadership characteristics associated with all three preferences and your unique make-up. Understanding this allows you to develop and benefit from your ability to use self-knowledge to make wise choices about how you lead and influence others.

THE PARTICIPATIVE LEADER

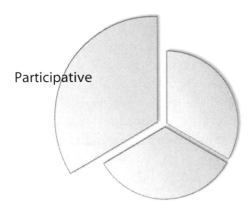

Participative

Mark Aardsma, the founder and CEO of ATS Acoustics, is an example of a participative leader. He told me that he had moved his office to the second floor of his company's building. This separated him somewhat from his team members. From all appearances, Mark likes to be engaged with and spend time with people. He strives to be engaged with his employees and build relationships. Historically, he has spent a good deal of time close to the company's operations. While he is very capable, has a high degree of business acumen, and possesses strong analytic skills, his passion for business is grounded in a desire to spend time working with and coaching people. His workspace had always been close to the employees he worked with.

I wasn't surprised that he wasn't sure if he liked the change because he really hadn't spent any time in his new office. Apparently, when he came into the building each morning, he immediately began engaging and working with the employees on the shop floor. Since I've known Mark, he has become increasingly aware of the value of directly coaching his employees. He finds it a wonderful way to increase their capabilities, and it has resulted in a higher level of delegation. Mark advocates teamwork among his employees and believes that the one unique thing his company delivers to its customers is an extraordinarily high level of customer service. He believes so strongly in being responsive that the company does not use an automated phone system—no recorded voice or set of prompts and choices—and it doesn't take more than a couple of rings for someone to answer a call. Mark's belief in the value of giving attention to the customer is unwavering.

Several weeks after the move to his new office, Mark told me that he liked having the space to do one-on-one coaching with employees and was holding meetings there. He even added more furniture and arranged his office to accommodate the meetings. The traits and characteristics of participative leadership are ground in inclusion and attention. The participative leader prefers high levels of team and group interaction that require team members to work closely together. This results in a high degree of communication, information sharing and social interaction. Often, participative leaders refer to their companies as one big family and create environments that motivate and encourage interaction. They enjoy the idea of community and feel that connection is a key to success.

Participative leaders are good team builders and facilitators of group environments, assuring that individual members of the group or team feel included, paid attention to, and listened to. If someone is not participating, the leader will intentionally invite the person to get engaged or ask for their comments. They further accomplish this by asking each person for input. Emotionally, the worst thing that can happen is for someone to feel left out.

Participative leaders show a preference for planning and strategizing that is group focused with a high level of involvement, broad participation, and often brainstorming. They emphasize diversity, shared problem solving, and often push for consensus, unanimous, and concordance-based decision making. When it comes to a company vision, mission, and strategy, they prefer to draw in the group to articulate it, which is also a way to ensure their involvement. They often rely on group members to do the more detailed work. Shared reward is often the preferred approach of participative leaders, and group outcomes are frequently treated as more important than individual accomplishments. At a company level, this often leads to profit sharing and group celebrations. For some participative leaders, the goal is to create an ESOP or employee stock owned company. Participative leaders often focus on finding win-win solutions and outcomes to conflict and frequently include all members of a team or group in the process.

At times, they will work to accommodate or include another person's point of view. The participative leader will often rely on building goodwill and trust in relationships, leveraging the power of relationships over the power derived from the use of granted authority or rank or individual expertise. Their key motivation is the desire to provide others with a sense of significance, self-worth, and inclusion.

Participative leaders naturally show a preference for product or service strategies that offer a high degree of attention to the customer and promote connection and community. The idea of spending time with customers is important, as is bringing customers together. Often, they gravitate toward partnerships, joint ventures, and sharing strategies and ideas, including the possibilities of cooperative competition.

Their potential weaknesses, challenges, and criticisms include a desire to engage in too many meetings, to invite too much collaboration resulting in too slow decision making, to fail to take a stand to confront difficult situations and conflict when necessary, and to overlook group dysfunction, preferring to overharmonize or maintain the status quo. They may not share negative information or confront lapses in individual responsibility, accountability, or team performance. They may also fail to create detailed and measurable goals in planning and strategies and not offer enough structure and clarity in defining measurable objectives and outcomes, often overlooking details and timelines.

At their best, they work to assure that a high level of teamwork, communication, and information sharing takes place. This extends itself outward and is not lost on the customer. Edgar Huber, the CEO of Lands' End, once told me that an important aspect of his role is to build a bridge for communication across the company. That's a good description of a participative leader.

THE EXPERT LEADER

Rick Whipple is driven to achieve and accomplish the extraordinary. When something is mundane and without risk, he's looking for the next possibility. Throughout his life, and in his business, he pursues excellence. In his view, everything a person undertakes has challenges, or an element of something they don't like. Rick loves being in business and enjoys its intellectual aspects. He likes the challenge of finding new and better ways to do things, including how to lead his company. If he didn't, he'd probably be bored. To Rick, WhippleWood is much more than a business. It is a pursuit of possibilities, which is why he believes that while expertise and competency are the most important aspects of the company's capability, it's a matter of finding them in the right people. He competes in an industry that demands you be different to be better. He illustrates the expert leader.

There are approximately 35,000 CPA firms in the United States; approximately 500 are as large or larger than WhippleWood. They all hire really good people. Yet most don't get to be among the biggest and don't grow. Rick doesn't think those other companies are hiring the right people. Any firm, large or small, can get competent employees. For Whipple-Wood, it's about finding a certain type of individual.

In 2007, in the face of the coming recession, his firm took the risk of buying the building it currently occupies. In the heart of the recession, 2008, he began adding employees and continued growing the business. At that time, Rick recognized the need to bring aspects of teaming into the business. He didn't want the culture that is typically associated with accounting firms; he wanted it be unique and to buck the trend. He took his employees on a retreat and, building on its momentum, in four years, the firm doubled in size. As he sees it, the company's now annual retreats are critical to its success. He believes that when you determine the key aspects of the business and continue to focus on them, they become a part of your culture. The outcomes of the first retreat included WhippleWood's statement of purpose, the articulation of its values, and its business strategy, including designing the firm's structure, identifying its ideal customers, and strategizing how it would engage with clients.

They also established five "Champion Groups." People choose what group to participate in and, if they want to, can switch. The groups allow employees to pursue individual interests and strengths. The individual groups focus on five pursuits:

- Great Work Environment.
- Our People (improving performance; it uses a balanced score card with five measurements).

- Standards, Processes, and Technology (improving the mechanics of the firm and how things get done, including data management, which is key to an accounting firm).
- Our Clients (developing relationships with clients including qualifying them, managing which clients they want and don't want). The firm turns away more clients than it accepts.
- Marketing and Business Development (community involvement, tracking the business pipeline, etc.).

The groups' purpose is to provide unique elements that integrate participation into the company's culture of expertise and that allows employees to directly affect the company in positive ways. In Rick's view, people work at WhippleWood because they want to, not because it's a job. WhippleWood's employees work in an industry that, at certain times of the year, puts pressure on everyone. This makes its unique culture that much more important. WhippleWood employees are happy, focused, and hard working. They are also informal with one another. Monday mornings everyone gathers for a meeting, and they watch an inspirational or subject matter video. The person that chose the weekly video explains why, and everyone then shares something they found relevant or significant in their work and lives. People are very open in what they share, which they call "moments of happiness."

These are all conscious elements that help integrate participation and authenticity into the company's expertise culture. They add uniqueness to a culture well aligned to WhippleWood's brand intention of preeminence, which has many of the trademark characteristics of an expertise culture. Employees are measured on how they build on their individual performance and set goals and outcomes going forward. These include metrics for the amount of work people do and how it is billed; client generation; self-improvement; and the reconciliation of what each does for the firm. Employees design their personal education and learning plans and their career paths.

Rick Whipple's influence on his company's culture is apparent. His goal is to rely on his influence more than his authority. Based on people's competency and capability, he likes delegating decision making. He is committed to leading a company that is dynamic, exciting, and fun. He also recognizes that he may have to push people harder to get to where they want to go and that they are ready to respond.

Rick believes that if you have the skills, you can go wherever you want to go. The single biggest challenge is getting the most competent people to lead his firm in the future. Regardless of how long they stay and where they eventually go, he wants employees to look back on their experience at WhippleWood and say, "That was great, I used to work there."

Rick is an example of an expert leader who has a great sense of his own influence and wants to find the uniqueness in himself and his company. He also has the valuable capability to integrate aspects of the other leadership styles, which allows him to intentionally create a unique culture for his company.

Expert leaders typically prefer taking control of situations and dominating team environments, challenging team members to demonstrate individual competency and responsibility. They are seen as preferring organization, functional role definition, and a sense of hierarchy. Often, they try to influence team members' ideas and are seen as persuasive, regularly using analytical approaches, factual data, and statistical evidence in demonstrating their point of view. In conflict, this often results in a win-lose approach.

Expert leaders typically take an analytical approach to planning. They are often considered visionaries. Characteristically, their visioning process relies on their analytical capability. When it comes to risk, they will either work from a place of knowing or affirming belief in the potential outcome outweighing the potential downside. Expert leaders see themselves as resilient and persistent in reaching their objective and goals.

Expert leaders naturally prefer meritocratic forms of reward and rarely show empathy for those making mistakes. In solving problems and making decisions, they typically rely on team members who offer the highest level of expertise and knowledge and will often engage individual experts from outside the team and organization. They often create competitive environments, looking for the "best and brightest" team members to "step up" and compete with one another. They are seen as challenging the status quo and being innovative, consistently seeking continuous improvements in processes and systems and better outcomes. The key motivation of expert leaders is their desire to appear competent and in control and to leverage their knowledge and expertise, as well as that of others.

Strategically and when engaging customers, expert leaders prefer to lead the way. Creating solutions and finding answers internally and externally is their specialty, whether it's solving problems or developing products or services. Expert leaders often convey a "we will build it and they will come" attitude and are seen as driven by innovation and futuristic ideals.

The potential weaknesses, challenges, and criticisms of expert leaders include the desire to overcontrol an environment, dictate the actions of others, and centralize decision making, as well as an inability to effectively delegate responsibilities, authority, and power. They often find solutions to problems and reach decisions faster than most people, which keeps them from gaining the opinions and insights of others. This may leave team members feeling unheard, ignored, and unrecognized for their competency and expertise. Members may feel that the leader is too strongly influencing their ideas, resulting in a future lack of input and healthy discourse.

Expert leaders can be seen as creating overly critical environments, often suggesting that the performance of others, despite their accomplishments, may not be good enough. This may result in others feeling a lack of recognition. While challenging others can have its benefits, expert leaders can easily fall into patterns of behavior associated with a "must win" attitude and appear to need to always be right. Because expert leaders commonly believe that improvement is always possible, they may create new and multiple strategies at a pace that leaves followers confused.

Expert leaders place a great deal of importance on finding the right people for the right job. This creates a reliance on not just hiring competent employees with expertise, it also requires a commitment to training and development. This also extends to the development of competent leadership.

Over the last decade, the story of the North American Division of Ensign Energy reads like a guide to leadership alignment. Since 2001, when its management team strategized its alignment, the organization's assets have multiplied over 250 times. By 2013, as a result of its drive to deliver new technologies, it has grown from a little over 100 employees to over 2,800.

The keys to its alignment include a clearly defined strategic path to providing superior technology and customer service, a well-articulated and aligned culture of expertise and competency, and consistent leadership. For most of the past decade, the division has been led by Tom Schledwitz, who espouses values centered on finding people who are the right fit for the culture, relentlessly investing in their training and building career paths. For Tom, it's all about the people. He wants leadership that is more about communicating the intention and the outcome than being prescriptive.

To him, success comes from hiring and training the right people who will develop the right programs and processes. Tom looks for people with an entrepreneurial flair who are more apt to want to contribute and make things happen. He advocates freedom over compliance, wanting people to express themselves rather than being reactive and working within a program. He believes that good leadership is about managing a process without micromanaging people or taking away their creativity and accountability. He believes a good leader has high integrity, which is a key focus of leadership in the division's culture, and looks for leaders who know the core values are and can consistently communicate them to others. Tom also believes that a good leader is aware of what he doesn't know; a bad leader is only aware of what he does know.

Tom Schledwitz is a great example of an expert leader focused on building people's expertise, competency, and know-how. Like Rick Whipple, Tom believes it's always about the right people. In addition, both want to be innovative and unique; to be challenged and to challenge others; and to help others develop, grow and be successful. Further, they want their employees to be responsible and to take action that best delivers to the customer. Last, they both have a great deal of influence on their respective cultures.

THE SERVANT LEADER

Servant

When Dr. Carl Clark became CEO of the Mental Health Center of Denver (MHCD) in 2000, the organization was unprofitable. It had struggled with the implementation of business disciplines and a lack of clarity in its mission and vision. While the Center was delivering services to those in need, it was struggling to find a consistent way to operate, put financial disciplines in place, clearly articulate its culture, and build the relationships necessary for sustainability and growth. Clark's approach is that of the servant leader.

In the past, the Center's problems had been smoothed over, and one of Carl's first challenges was to confront and begin addressing some of the more critical and longstanding issues. In particular, he had to find ways to better assess and measure the Center's performance, including its systems and processes, as well as its outcomes in helping those who were coming to MHCD for services. Before alignment, he needed employees to buy into in the effort. In an organization focused on creating individual empowerment, getting everyone moving in the same direction isn't easy.

Carl's first engaged the members of his board and leadership team in clearly defining the mission of the Center and then to articulate a strategy, one that would require significant change. When it comes to creating and leading change, it is often best to use what is already present in the culture to leverage the change it needs to create. Carl asked everyone—the board members, leadership team, and all the employees—to act in the best interest of those they served. He consistently communicated that the only way to help others was to first commit to helping the Center by undertaking the operational changes required. He focused on doing more of the good work the Center prided itself on; his priority was the care of consumers, and the only way to get there was to focus on implementing aligned operational capabilities, business disciplines, and a healthy culture. He engaged everyone in a vision that focused on the creation and implementation of cutting edge approaches to mental health care and that led to its clients living healthy, productive, and meaningful lives. This was a greater and more compelling vision than just providing care.

Carl engaged everyone in the conversation, including the community. He strove to include everyone in the conversation and worked tirelessly to work in service and dedication to the Center. The resulting mission of MHCD is *enriching lives and minds by focusing on strengths and recovery.* For servant leaders like Carl, the source of their power and influence is to role model and reinforce the idea of helping others to succeed by making them better. He recognized that everything coming together required an aligned culture. Therefore, part of the Center's mission was to create a wellness culture within the organization, establishing a work environment where people can do what they do best, be supported, and enjoy their work.

To assure that the Center had aligned leadership, Carl provided training and education to those in leadership roles. They underwent extensive development; each had individual long term goals and outcomes. The Center built a new facility and received the highest Leadership in Energy and Environmental Design (LEED®) Platinum Certification from the U.S. Green Building Council (USGBC). It has received numerous awards for its recovery programs and for bringing mental health care into the national conversation. Carl has testified before Congress on behalf of mental health and, as one of the foremost recognized leaders in the field, has become a nationally recognized resource for its advancement. In the span of a decade, MHCD has become the model for other mental healthcare organizations.

For servant leaders, like Carl, the primary motivation is helping others. Over the last several decades, this preference has received greater recognition and attention. While servant leaders are often considered less competitive than others, it is not true. As with Carl Clark or John

McKay of Whole Foods, they can be very competitive and achievement oriented, yet they, like participative and expert leaders, have a unique way of achieving their goals.

Servant leaders prefer empowering and enabling others and building commitment to the purpose, cause, or ideal. They are developers and nurturers of others. They are stewards of the people and organization. They typically derive their influence from their alignment to a set of values and beliefs that inspire people to create change. They are charismatic and pursue a high-level purpose and vision; they are seen as authentic and caring.

Servant leaders prefer less structure and measurement and are inclined to encourage others to define their own goals, motivating them through intrinsic rewards and opportunities for self-actualization and contribution. They often express the belief that mistakes and errors are an expected part of the learning process.

Servant leaders are often able to build close personal relationships and create warm, friendly environments. They are comfortable with the emotions and feelings of team members and followers. When confronting conflict, they are open to new ideas and diverse points of view. They prefer resolutions and outcomes that reflect "the right thing to do." Their key motivation is to be liked, loved, and admired and to leverage the good intention of others.

Servant leaders show a strong tendency to pursue customer experiences that deliver wellbeing, personal growth, and forms of enrichment, which are natural extensions of their own curiosity and desire to grow and self-actualize. They are often described as generous and humanitarian people, who encourage others to pursue causes. Despite their unassuming demeanor, their charismatic energy often puts them at the center of their companies. Potential weaknesses, challenges, and criticisms of servant leaders are a lack of direction and their potential to underemphasize measurable outcomes and performance. Therefore, they are thought to focus more on intention than results, ignore concrete and objective data, and minimize the need for strategy and planning. They may be considered too optimistic, and their inspirational style can burn out team members. Because they desire to help others grow and succeed, they can easily overcommit and miss deadlines and, because they want to be liked and don't want to let others down, it is difficult for them to say "no."

THE ALIGNMENT OF LEADERSHIP

An aligned leader's orientation is a reliable indicator of why individual leaders prefer specific brand intentions and how they pursue advancement and innovation. Understanding this benefits them and their groups.

Figure 10.1 illustrates how important leadership alignment is to the success of any company, as well as team leaders themselves. The level of success is a direct outcome of an individual's alignment to the company's market strategy. Thus, participative leaders generally succeed best in pursuit of the brand intentions of customization and community; experts in pursuit of low price and preeminence; and servants in the pursuit of physical wellbeing and personal actualization. For the same reasons, partners, leadership teams, boards of directors, and leaders within any organization or team can easily have differing views on the wide range of possibilities that relate to the basic what, why, and how of the business.

Human Motivation	Customer Motivation	Brand Intention	Culture Preference	Leadership Preference
To feel important	Attention	Community	Participation	Participative
		Customization		
To feel competent	Competency	Preeminence	Expertise	Expert
		Low Price		
To feel accepted	Caring	Physical Wellbeing	Authenticity	Servant
		Personal Actualization		

Figure 10.1 The Alignment of Leadership

WHEN LEADERS AREN'T ALIGNED

There are a variety of reasons why a leader may not be aligned to the cultures for which they are responsible, including poor succession planning, poor hiring practices, and a lack of clarity about the desired leadership approach. There are several approaches to this problem. The first is for the leader to assess the misalignment and choose behavior that allows integration into the existing culture. An expert leader, who realizes she is leading a participative group rather than making decisions on behalf of the team or getting the advice of one particular member, should hold meetings to reach consensus decisions. A servant leader in an expertise culture realizes that one of the company's better clients is not getting the level of service they expect. Typically, he would let his team know about the issue and expect someone to empower himself to resolve it. Instead, to better align to the culture, he goes to the individual responsible for that customer or, based on what the customer needs, goes to the person whose role it is, and asks that person to respond. He will also meet with the employee to discuss how to avoid a similar situation in the future.

For a leader, whose style and approach is misaligned to a culture, to successfully integrate requires the flexibility to choose behaviors that will create alignment as well as a high level of self-knowledge and a keen awareness of the range of potential situations they may have to confront. Many leaders have had success doing this by hard work and commitment.

The second approach occurs when a leader decides it is best to change the culture. Because this always has a significant effect on a company or team, the most effective and expedient approach is to replace people. An exception is when the company has a culture it aspires to, has already aligned several of the keys, and is working toward increased alignment. In that case, it is more about further aligning and improving an existing culture than about a complete change of preference.

The third approach occurs when a leader's preference differs from the culture's, and he is unwilling to align to it. He can try to influence a change in the company's culture, yet if, over time, the strategy fails and he still won't change his behavior and leadership style, he must leave, willingly or unwillingly.

The fourth option is to "get out of their own way." For example, as part of the succession plan of a family business, the daughter of the founder, at his retirement, took over the company's day-to-day operations and leadership. Her father was a very outgoing participative leader who created a family-like culture. The daughter was a more reserved expert leader, who enjoyed the analytic nature of the business.

She quickly realized how misaligned and different her approach was from her father's. Rather than disrupt the business or take on the challenge and risk of changing her own approach, she turned over the day-to-day leadership to one of the managers whose style aligned to the existing culture. When she attended meetings, she was intentional and very conscientious about not taking over or interfering with the company's participative planning and decision making processes.

In addition to influencing a company's culture, leaders influence the strategic thinking process. In this last example, the daughter needed not only to be aware of her influence on the culture and *how* things were done, she also had to be aware of her influence on the strategy and the *what* and *why* of the company.

ELEVEN

Actions for Alignment

Change and growth are the result of striving for self- knowledge and realizing our choices.

I once joined a multinational company to assist in a global rebranding effort. The company had 12,000 employees worldwide. Although the majority of its employees worked in North America, it had an operations or sales presence in a host of nations around the world. The team charged with the rebranding effort discovered that not everyone was as committed to the strategy as those at headquarters. My task was to help facilitate the conversation to align everyone to the effort and move the rebranding forward across the international group.

While the company's culture leaned toward expertise, it never clearly articulated this or communicated it well across the company. It had a vague set of values established at its inception several years' prior, yet not much attention had been paid to it as the company rapidly grew. This resulted in misaligned practices and mixed messages. There were also a number of subcultures, particularly in its technical facility in France and several European marketing and sales offices.

The executive responsible for the project realized that the branding effort would only work if it aligned to the culture. While the logo was already chosen and aspects of the brand management project were well underway, the further the company moved down the path toward the international rollout, the more the misalignments surfaced. This was very apparent in relation to the description of the new brand narrative. The executive, realizing this, took the initiative and began a conversation to align everyone to the new brand identity. He scheduled a multiday meeting in Europe and invited representatives from all over the world to attend and participate in the conversation. The meeting was designed to create alignment to the effort. While it might not satisfy everyone, it would assure that the worldwide branding and marketing efforts were aligned and the effort would succeed.

At the meeting, I began by asking four very simple questions about the rebranding effort: What's working? What isn't working? What does this tell us? And, what is needed to create success?

Answers to the first question included comments about the new logo, which they agreed was a big improvement, insights into how it would be perceived, and their appreciation that someone was asking them for input.

The list of answers to the second question was much longer. It included comments about the lack of communication, lack of involvement, lack of any exchange of ideas—rebranding was just another directive and some of the language used would not work well in Japan and Italy, and so on.

We then explored what this was telling us and talked about alignment and how to successfully manage the challenge of the change. We also discussed their emotional response to the change, the transition they were undergoing, and what was important to them going forward. The executive leading the effort did a remarkable job listening, asking questions and helping to create an openness required for the exchange of ideas. In an expertise culture, it's good to ask the experts for their insights. By the end of the first day, the energy was shifting, and ideas were beginning to emerge. On the second day, the group took on the fourth question, collaborating to create a strategy, identifying the priorities for immediate implementation, and setting a plan for the worldwide effort.

An added benefit was the insight the group generated about the company's misaligned culture, which also increased their understanding of its subcultures and how to better manage them relative to the company's expertise culture. Within 18 months, the company gathered 300 of its key leaders at a leadership summit, where they identified the company's core values and aligned its leadership and its culture to its brand.

It is always valuable to pay attention to what the members of the team or organization communicate about what's working and what's not. It provides insight into what alignments are present and where the misalignments are.

GOING FORWARD

Inevitably, alignment begins at the top, with leadership's commitment and pursuit of the goal. The responsibility and accountability resides with them.

As the example demonstrates, any part of an organization or any individual team at any level can take the initiative to align. It will greatly benefit the work of that particular team or group and should be communicated and shared with the company's leadership.

Companies with boards of directors should make sure they are part of the process. When a board of directors or advisory board is misaligned, it can have a domino effect throughout the organization. The purpose of board members is to benefit a company by presenting their points of view based on their experience, expertise, and individual wisdom. An aligned board can be powerfully productive.

How to go about aligning a company or team is in the framework. Examining how different cultures plan and organize will provide insight into the approach that will give you the best result. Trust the process and remember that the best way to effect change is by leveraging what is already present in the culture.

First, familiarize yourself with the system for alignment. Begin to assess the business and identify the opportunities for alignment. Identify who in the organization should participate. Answering this question may provide immediate insight into your culture and leadership's orientation. Next, begin the process of assessing and creating your alignment strategies. The pursuit of alignment forces you to ask the difficult questions and confront thorny issues and sacred cows. It also provides ample opportunity to determine what new strategies fit and to weed out those that will likely not work. This will save time and resources and create trust in leadership.

One of the greatest outcomes of the pursuit of alignment is leadership development. Typically, this focuses on individual facets and competencies of leadership. When leaders work to align an organization or team, they are engaged in all aspects of leadership and develop an integrated set of competencies.

After engaging in the pursuit of alignment, we are better at identifying other possibilities. Embedding alignment as part of your vision and culture delivers higher levels of performance and competitive capability and increases your ability to win.

At the outset of this book, I shared my observation that alignment is the greatest challenge facing companies and their leaders. To be successful in leading aligned teams and organizations requires ongoing focus, continuous assessment, and the desire and will to confront misalignments. To be successful, the leaders of companies and their members must be willing to engage in the ongoing conversation of alignment—and to do so in an honest and open fashion. As you have likely already concluded, *alignment is the conversation.* As I offered at the outset of this book, *welcome to the conversation.*

TRUE ALIGNMENT
ASSESSMENT

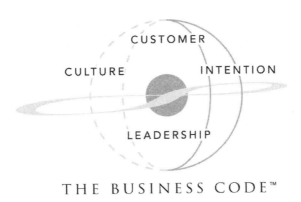

Alignment has long been the greatest challenge of leadership. Its importance, along with its effect on performance, has only increased over time. Today, to come close to competing and succeeding in the chaotic and rapidly shifting business environment, leaders must create aligned teams and organizations. For extraordinary companies—those that consistently compete and win in the marketplace—the overriding characteristic that is invariably present and separates them from their competition is alignment.

The Business Code is a framework for alignment that can be applied to any organization or team regardless of its size. It provides a proven approach to confront and overcome the challenges of misalignment. The Business Code reveals the insights needed to create strategies and initiatives and take actions that result in the alignment required to compete and achieve high levels of organizational and team performance.

There are four elements to this systemic approach: *the customer, intention, culture,* and *leadership.* Through these four elements, the framework provides a measurable and observable means of articulating and aligning a company or team to customer expectations. The Business Code provides a comprehensive lens through which to view the patterns of behavior through cultures that can be intentionally led. It provides a systemic approach to aligning internal behavior (how a company's or team's members engage each other) to external behavior (how they engage the customer).

The four elements of alignment make up the Business Code:

The Customer: Narrowly defined, *a customer is the person who pays for your product or service.* Broadly defined, *a customer is any person who buys and receives or is affected by your product or service.*

Intention: *Intention is the thoughtful and deliberate delivery, through a product or service, of a promise to the customer. Brand intention reflects the quality of purposefulness through which the product or service is delivered.*

Culture: *Culture defines how people treat one another, including the patterns and norms of behavior that members engage in at individual and group levels to achieve success. Culture defines acceptable and unacceptable behavior.*

Leadership: When joined with the other elements of the Business Code, leaders have incredible influence and often hold the key to alignment. As complex as the study of leadership is, the most straightforward definition is *influencing others to act.* Leaders are responsible for acting in a manner that clearly conveys how the intention of the business is implemented and, ultimately, how the customer is treated. They are responsible for role modeling, reinforcing and, in the final analysis, living the reputation of the companies or teams they lead.

The first step to alignment is assessing its current level throughout a company or team. Once this is accomplished, the gaps can be readily identified and specific strategies developed and implemented. For the ongoing alignment process, periodic assessment may be applied to track improvement, as well as ongoing deficiencies, and to determine how the trends are impacting performance.

For the purpose of conducting such an assessment, the following questions provide insight into the alignment of the company or the team and its members. The questions are derived from this book and the four elements of the Business Code, and they offer the opportunity to explore specific strategies and behaviors. The assessment can be used at an individual, team, department, division, or company-wide level. Regardless of the level of involvement in the assessment process, one of the key outcomes is the exploration of, and engagement in, the conversation about alignment.

Each question asks for a response on a scale ranging from 1 (poorly) to 6 (effectively). The following is a guide to further interpretation of this scale:

1 There is no evidence of this characteristic of alignment.
2 There is very little, if any, evidence of this characteristic.
3 There is some evidence of this characteristic. It is inconsistent and lacks clarity. There is significant opportunity for alignment.
4 There is increased evidence of this characteristic of alignment. Occasional misalignment prevents increased performance.
5 There is a significant level of alignment. There is still some room for furthering alignment and increased performance.
6 We are very well aligned. There is little, if any, room for improvement.

The scale results in two significant outputs. The first is the ability to calculate an average score among participants contributing to the assessment. This allows for the identification of the traits and characteristics that present the greatest strengths of and challenges to a team or company. Second, the assessment provides a range of responses for each characteristic. This allows for engagement in the inquiry and conversation focusing on the perceptions and experiences of individual members and the causes of their varying viewpoints. Exploring the differences in individual perspectives can often offer powerful insights that result in meaningful strategies for the alignment of a team or company. As with any diagnostic and assessment tool, individual perspectives, definitions, and experiences may vary. For this reason, it is valuable to refer to the text of this book as a reference.

	Poorly				Effectively	
1. How well is our purpose articulated and communicated to our customers?	1	2	3	4	5	6
2. How aligned is the communication of our purpose to our team members and employees?	1	2	3	4	5	6
3. How aligned to our customers' expectations are our products and services?	1	2	3	4	5	6
4. How well aligned are we in satisfying the concerns and challenges of our customers and keeping our promises to them?	1	2	3	4	5	6
5. How well do we listen to our customers?	1	2	3	4	5	6
6. How well is our vision articulated and understood?	1	2	3	4	5	6
7. How well is our brand intention articulated and understood by everyone?	1	2	3	4	5	6
8. How aligned are our present and future product and service strategies to our brand intention?	1	2	3	4	5	6
9. How engaged are members of our team and company in contributing to our brand intention?	1	2	3	4	5	6
10. How well are our marketing strategies aligned to our brand intention?	1	2	3	4	5	6
11. How well are our selling and delivery processes aligned to our brand intention?	1	2	3	4	5	6

	Poorly			*Effectively*		
12. How well is our unique recipe articulated and understood by everyone?	1	2	3	4	5	6
13. How well do we focus on short-term goals in alignment to our vision and long-term goals?	1	2	3	4	5	6
14. How aligned to the brand intention are present and future operational strategies?	1	2	3	4	5	6
15. How well aligned are team goals to the company's vision and goals?	1	2	3	4	5	6
16. How well is our culture articulated and understood by everyone?	1	2	3	4	5	6
17. How well are our shared values and beliefs aligned and communicated to everyone?	1	2	3	4	5	6
18. How well are people held responsible for the alignment of their behavior to our culture and its shared values and beliefs?	1	2	3	4	5	6
19. How well is an aligned approach to decision-making understood and used?	1	2	3	4	5	6
20. How well are our planning processes aligned with our culture?	1	2	3	4	5	6
21. How aligned are we in our approaches and processes to problem solving?	1	2	3	4	5	6
22. How well are individual roles defined and aligned to how things really get done?	1	2	3	4	5	6

	Poorly				*Effectively*	
23. How aligned are we in how conflict is managed and resolved?	1	2	3	4	5	6
24. How aligned to our culture are our approaches to incentive and reward?	1	2	3	4	5	6
25. How well defined and aligned are our approaches to goal setting?	1	2	3	4	5	6
26. How well defined and aligned are our hiring processes?	1	2	3	4	5	6
27. How well is our approach to leadership development aligned to our culture?	1	2	3	4	5	6
28. How well is our definition of teamwork articulated and understood?	1	2	3	4	5	6
29. How well do the cultures of our teams align to the culture of the organization?	1	2	3	4	5	6
30. How well are the behaviors of team members aligned to a shared definition of teamwork?	1	2	3	4	5	6
31. How well do leaders act in alignment with our culture?	1	2	3	4	5	6
32. How well do the leaders address issues of responsibility and accountability?	1	2	3	4	5	6
33. How well do team members give and receive feedback from one another?	1	2	3	4	5	6
34. How well do team members demonstrate their commitment and trust to one another?	1	2	3	4	5	6

	Poorly				*Effectively*	
35. How well do team members listen to each other?	1	2	3	4	5	6
36. How well do team members share information and ideas with one another?	1	2	3	4	5	6
37. How well do leaders give and receive feedback?	1	2	3	4	5	6
38. How well do leaders confront conflict and disagreement?	1	2	3	4	5	6
39. How well does the organization perform candid self-assessment and understand its strengths and weaknesses?	1	2	3	4	5	6
40. How well does the team plan and and implement strategies for improving its alignment?	1	2	3	4	5	6

To increase the value of this assessment, consider the following questions.

⇒ Based on the assessment, what are the key strengths of the organization or team?

⇒ How can you increase your use of these strengths?

⇒ Based on the assessment, what are the areas and characteristics of alignment you need to improve?

⇒ What are the barriers and obstacles that may keep you from improving these?

⇒ What are your priorities in addressing the areas of improvement and becoming more aligned?

⇒ What strategies and actions will you undertake to increase your alignment and performance?

INDEX